# My Memoirs

By "ME" Lord Margaret Thatcher (ME) ☆

## CONTENTS

ILLUSTRATIONS :

FIG 1 - where I buried Stargar

PLATE 4 - the one I had
lunch with

PLUS :

why I am not mad —
see CHAPTER RADIATOR

GREAT COMPETITION :

win £50,000 in cash
in my GEOFFREY HOWE fatwa
challenge. THE END OF THE
BOOK ... AT THE BACK

REPRISE

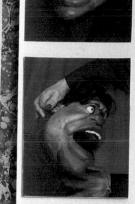

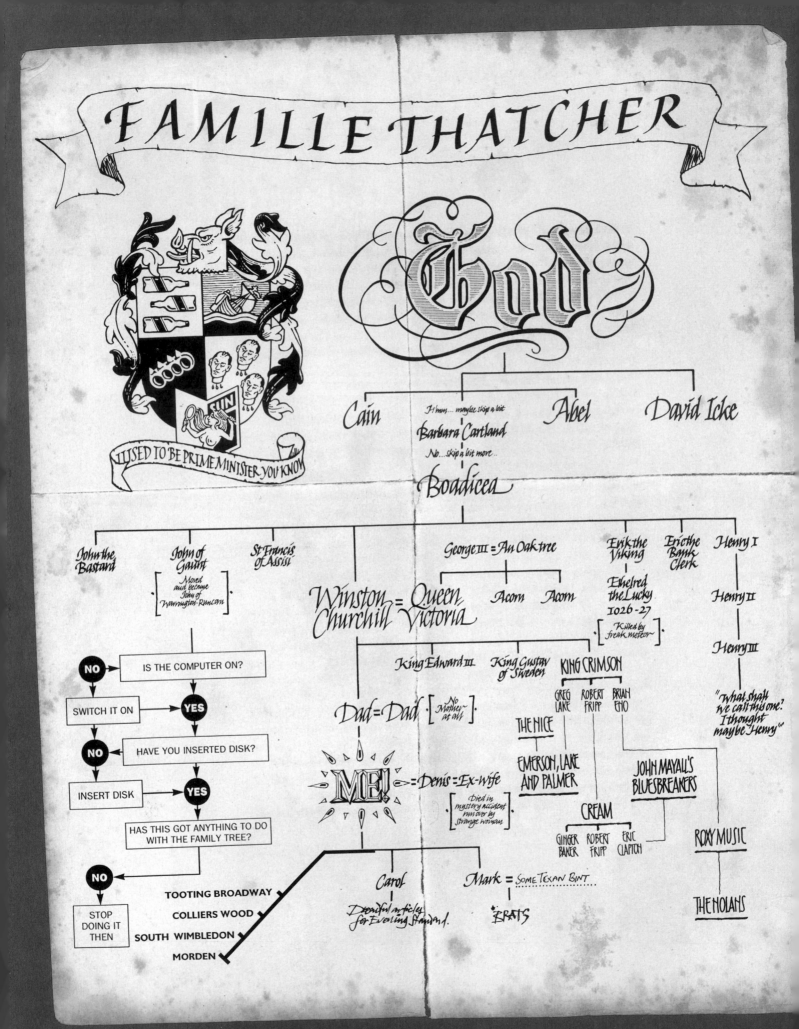

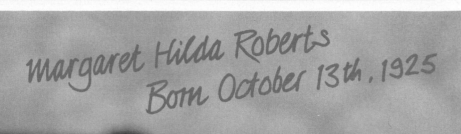

margaret Hilda Roberts
Born October 13th, 1925

## GRANTHAM
## GENERAL HOSPITAL
### Maternity Ward

Name of baby................MARGARET HILDA ROBERTS..................

Sex     Boy ☐     Girl ☐     ALIEN

Blood group   A ☐  B ☐  AB ☐  O ☐   CONCENTRATED ACID

Type of delivery.........UNEXPECTEDLY BURST THROUGH CHEST

Condition of mother.................VERY SURPRISED

Uncle Ted. We don't like to talk about him. A
I remember is he used to always give us ants
Christmas.

Ebeneezer Thatcher - A model of the Victorian
entrepreneur. He owned a number of profitable
mills in the North West and was famous for supplying
his workers with a wide range of interests they
could pursue outside of working hours - activities
such as more working in the mill, doing an extra
unpaid weekend shift in the mill, being tied for
seventeen years to the mill. He eventually left
Lancashire as he said he wished to take up a
missionary position in Africa.

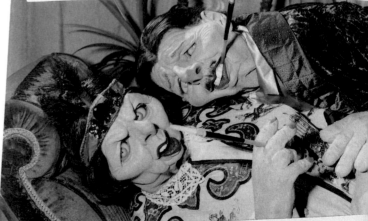

W.G. Thatcher - the perfect cricketer.
Some people thought the long beard to be a
bit out of place, but I think it rather
suited her. Author of "Cricket Bats and
Their Uses - A guide to Foreign Diplomacy".
Also an accomplished bowler, developing
the technique of swapping the ball for a
sharpened javelin.

Great Aunt Florence Thatcher - Aunt Florence
was the first woman to ever close a hospital.
By introducing an internal market into all
the Crimean field hospitals she discovered it
was cheaper to have the British injured
treated by the Russians. The only snag snag
being that they rather unsportingly refused
to give our soldiers back when they got
better.

Bertie and Arabella Thatcher.- bounder and flapper.
Poor Bertie lost his entire fortune in 1929. He
took all his money out of stocks and shares the day
before the crash but on the way home he popped into
a pub and bought a packet of cashew nuts. Arabella
was often to be found in the beds of celebrated
artists and musicians of the day until eventually
the police had a word with her and told her to stop
breaking into people's houses. She died a bitter
woman having never forgiven Isadora Duncan for
ruining her scarf.

n Von Thatcher – World War I flying ace. Winner
the Iron Cross and hero of the Kaiser's Germany
shooting down over a hundred British Tommies.
only blemish on his record was that he was supposed
be on the British side. Eventually shot down
self when the 'Carpets-U-like' banner he was
iling made him easier to spot.

Wesley Luther Thatcher – son of Ebeneezer. Rarely
commented upon in family circles – his swarthy
complexion was presumed to be the result of a
mysterious illness probably caught in Africa off one
of Ebeneezer's many young nubile servants.

Reggie and Ronnie Thatcher – legitimate businessmen.
Great upholders of the Thatcher belief of "helping
yourself" and helped themselves all over the East
End. Loved the great outdoors and would disappear
at all hours to bury large bulky sacks in Epping
Forest. They were once accused of breaking the law
but this allegation was soon retracted although it
was hard to hear exactly what was said over the
noise of the cement mixor.

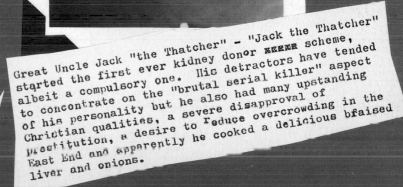

Great Uncle Jack "the Thatcher" – "Jack the Thatcher"
started the first ever kidney donor scheme,
albeit a compulsory one. His detractors have tended
to concentrate on the "brutal serial killer" aspect
of his personality but he also had many upstanding
Christian qualities, a severe disapproval of
prostitution, a desire to reduce overcrowding in the
East End and apparently he cooked a delicious braised
liver and onions.

## Eng

**England** (cont'd from last 400 pages) ...and gave the Spaniards a damn good hiding. Nowadays, the average Englishman is six foot tall with fine blue eyes, a ruddy complexion and a proud, jaunty expression. He is a tolerant, yet firm chap possessed of great meral fibre, and easily a match for the pitiful wretches that made up Kaiser Bill's Army. (cf **JOLLY OLD GREAT WAR**). England, to sum up, is therefore without doubt the most spiffing place on Earth, if not the entire Universe.

*Fig viii. A typical Englishman*

### Nature of country

| | |
|---|---|
| Top hole | |
| Good | |
| Reasonable | |
| Poor show | |

ENGLAND   ALL FOREIGNERS

*Fig ix. Scientific evidence of England's superioty*

**ETON** Fine old public school which has helped make **ENGLAND** (qv) great. Set up by Henry VI in 1440, who had a vision of "a seat of learning wherein shall be fashioned upper class twits who weareth stripey shirts and sayeth 'yarr excellent' a lot". Renowned for its harsh character-building regime: cold showers, random removal of limbs, etcetera. Developed the system of **FAGGING** – younger boys serving on older ones. Famous quote: "The Battle of Waterloo was won on the playing fields of Eton". Reference to Eton's favourite sport, which involved inviting thousands of French cavalry onto their playing fields and engaging them in hand to hand combat.

**EXCELLENCE** (quality of) Marvellous, perfect, super, jolly, whizzo, tickety-boo, top-hole, as in **ENGLAND** (qv)

**FOREIGNERS** Inferior people who have one thing in common; they don't live in **ENGLAND** (qv). Fall into three distinct groups:
i) Swarthy types, ruled over by an **EMPIRE** (qv), probably **ENGLAND's** (qv). Not to be trusted.
ii) Greasy Latin types whose once great civilisation was destroyed by unnatural sexual practices. (See **CAMBRIDGE UNIVERSITY**). Generally untrustworthy.
iii) Stiff Teutonic types with mad staring eyes – can't trust these. (Apart from that Hitler chap, he seems like a decent cove, if only he played cricket, at least he's made the trains run on time and let's face it, he's not likely to cause any trouble is he?)
If you see a foreigner, it is a good idea not to approach him, unless you are about to give him an order.

**FRENCH** See above. A ghastly arrogant race who think they're better than anyone else; not at all like the **ENGLISH** (qv). See also **WATERLOO; NAPOLEON; DAMN GOOD THRASHING; HA-HA.**

*Fig x. A typical Frenchman*

---

---

Handwritten notes (left side):

ii, 23/5/38.

of the common stick

onducted using Hoagkins ... to and two moths er

... put seperately into

... the legs with a pair of tweezers. ... thorax, using scalpel.

... ying glass was held above the beaker. ... ning of the outer membrane. ... tion of sulphuric acid (H2SO4) was ... d through a pipette having no legs. ... mors and fed into a mincer.

... quantify are pain threshord ... as they seem to die easily—

...gh study but what ...ith Geography?

---

# SCHOOL REPORT
# GRANTHAM GIRLS' GRAMMAR
Founded 18.55 (p.m.) Headmistress: Mrs M. Rutherford

Summer........ Term 1938

Name..Margaret..Hilda..Roberts

Form..3.2.....  Age..13½.

Absent....0..days..

| SUBJECT | GRADE | COMMENTS | INITIALS |
|---|---|---|---|
| MATHS | C | Mr Huggins is an average teacher, who simply refuses to listen. He really must learn to curb his arrogance and stop telling me to shut up, and get back in my seat! | M.H.R. |
| HISTORY | D | An appalling little man. Actually dared to suggest we could one day lose our Empire and that Africa used to be ruled by black people | M.H.R. |
| FRENCH | Z | monsieur Leblanc is a disgrace to the teaching profession. His lessons are not ever conducted in English. If he persists in this attitude, I will have no hesitation in sending him home | M.H.R. |
| GEOGRAPHY | A+ | An outstanding teacher, in every sense. He has taken a pay cut and accepted my proposals for a new curriculum. The most splendid teacher of Geography in the whole of...um, which country do we live in again? | M.H.R. |
| ART | | No thank-you. | M.H.R. |
| ENGLISH | E | I'm afraid Miss Harper has got a lot to learn about discipline; there's not nearly enough in her class. She doesn't reform her namby-pamby bleeding-heart liberal attitude I'm going to have to insist she canes me. | M.H.R. |
| SCIENCE | | Good, but Mr Hodgekinson really must spend more class time on weapons research. | M.H.R. |
| MUSIC | 4/4 | To save money, Miss Wimhurst's teaching contract should be... | M.H.R. |
| HANDICRAFTS | | | M.H.R. |

...mistress' comment......Aren't the teachers supposed to comment on her?

...of Parent..............................

Next term begins 3rd Sept. '38

---

---

---

## The Grantham Swimming Association
President: P. D. PHILE

# This is to certify

Margaret Hilda Roberts

managed two lengths of the Verucca Memorial Swimming Pool

STYLE  Walking

SIGNED  P.C.

DATE  3 June 1933

ISSUED BY THE GRANTHAM SWIMMING ASSOCIATION – For the promotion of physical and gymnastic excellence in the water and for the chance to ogle at nubile young girls cavorting in skimpy wet bathing suits and offer a brisk rub down with a towel... "Excuse me sir, I'm P.C. Collins, would you come with me please..."

**Young and In LOVE**

---

## Pin, Stripe & Cufflinks

SOLICITORS AND COMMISSIONERS FOR OATHS (*Whatever that means*)

Plush House,
Weir Avenue,
London W1G ON.

Dear Miss Roberts,

I am instructed by my client Mr Denis Thatcher, G.I.N. & BAR, that you have been harassing him with letters and certain telephone calls in which you informed him that he is, quote, "hung like a very small donkey". Also, he denies your claim that he "grabbed your hands with his lapels and pulled you into the ladies toilets for a snog". He is also unaware that he agreed to marry you. Come to think of it, he has been unaware of everything since Bank Holiday 1932.

You are hereby served with a Restraining Order under which you are instructed to remain a minimum distance of 500 yards from his house. You may under no circumstances leave his pet rabbit floating horribly boiled in his saucepan again.

Failure to comply will result in more incredibly dreary letters from us which are written in silly legal jargon which even we don't understand.

I remain, therein, your Most Obedient etcetera

---

**S.W.A.L.K**

Darling Mr Thatcher,

Thanks for last night. You were amazing on the dance floor. I've never seen anyone so .... unconscious. How romantic of you to let me drag you to the Young Conservatives Film Club. I loved "Foreigners are so funny". Oh Denis! You were so attractive in the moonlight. I'll never forget gazing for hours into your chequebook. You've got the most money I've ever seen. And you were magnificent, the way you intervened when that fight broke out. Next time leave your girlfriend at home. Better still leave her altogether. I want you to have my children,

margaret.

---

happen to like my girlfriend. Anyway
at dance? I don't remember anything
out a dance. Oh god think I'm gonna be sick

Denis

---

Roses are Red, Deadly Nightshade is Blue,
Either we're wed or I give some to *you*

Dear Denis,

I am sorry to hear about your girlfriend's disappearance next Tuesday. Imagine being struck by three javelins with poison tips! You'll be devastated and single again. Denis I want to be the man in your life. I'd like to help you in my hour of need. So let's meet. I know just the place. I'll meet you at St Bigot's church on Saturday at 3pm. Wear a suit. Don't be late or dig up your garden.

margaret.

---

My $uper $mashing Darling Denis,

I don't know what it is I ×××× love about you. It's been so wonderful seeing you every night. I think you saw *me* once, when you looked out the window; I was the one up the tree. Now I'm counting the days till I can see you again. In fact I'm marking it on the wall of my cell. They may have taken me from you, but I'll always treasure that lock of your hair - hope you didn't mind me pulling it out.

---

## HOTEL ANTHRAX

ISLE OF BLEAK
MILES OFF THE COAST OF SCOTLAND

Dear Anyone,

If you find this bottle, I am trapped on a remote island on a so-called 'honeymoon' with a mad young lady who insists that she is now my wife. So please, if anyone finds this bottle, could you fill it up with gin and return it.

Thanks awfully,
D. Thatcher

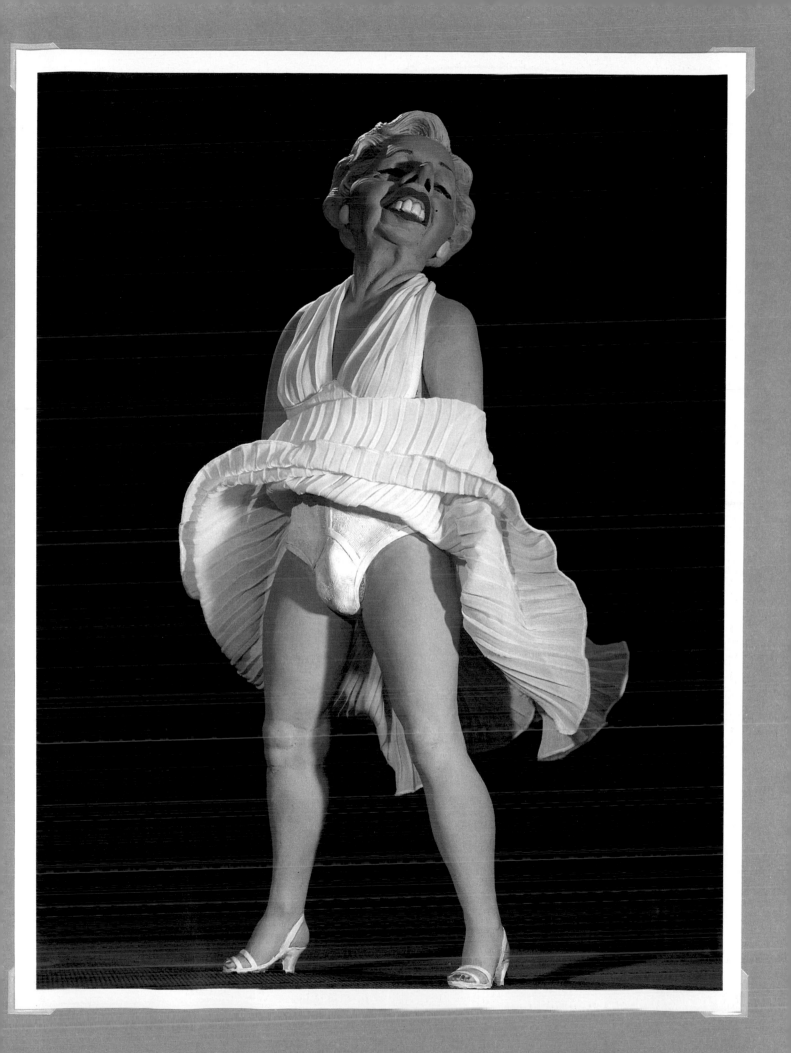

## ICE CREAM Mr SICKEE

BLOBBY-BITS HOUSE, QUEASY STREET
LONDON E107 (CARCINOGENIC)

*must remember this for later.*

Dear Margaret Roberts,

This is to confirm your appointment to our ice cream research department.

I'm afraid I won't be at the company when you start as I am being laid off following a management efficiency study which was anonymously sent in to the company shortly after I interviewed you. I believe Mr. Hargreaves already spoke to you about joining the Union. You'll be pleased to know he is now out of intensive care.

Yours sincerely,

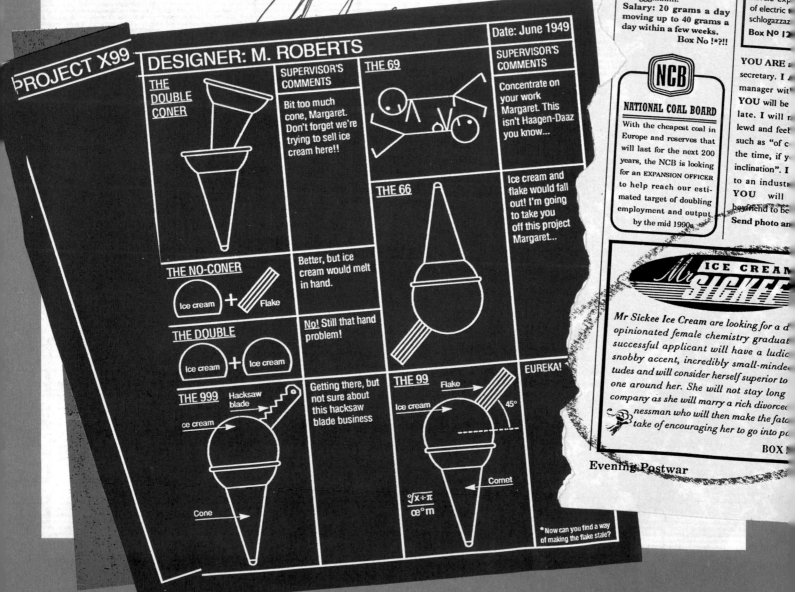

**PROJECT X99**

**DESIGNER: M. ROBERTS**

Date: June 1949

| | SUPERVISOR'S COMMENTS | | SUPERVISOR'S COMMENTS |
|---|---|---|---|
| **THE DOUBLE CONER** | Bit too much cone, Margaret. Don't forget we're trying to sell ice cream here!! | **THE 69** | Concentrate on your work Margaret. This isn't Haagen-Daaz you know... |
| **THE NO-CONER** Ice cream + Flake | Better, but ice cream would melt in hand. | **THE 66** | Ice cream and flake would fall out! I'm going to take you off this project Margaret... |
| **THE DOUBLE** Ice cream + Ice cream | No! Still that hand problem! | | |
| **THE 999** Hacksaw blade / ice cream / Cone | Getting there, but not sure about this hacksaw blade business | **THE 99** Flake / Ice cream / 45° / Cornet / $\sqrt[9]{x \div \pi}$ / œ°m / Cone | EUREKA! |

\* Now can you find a way of making the flake stale?

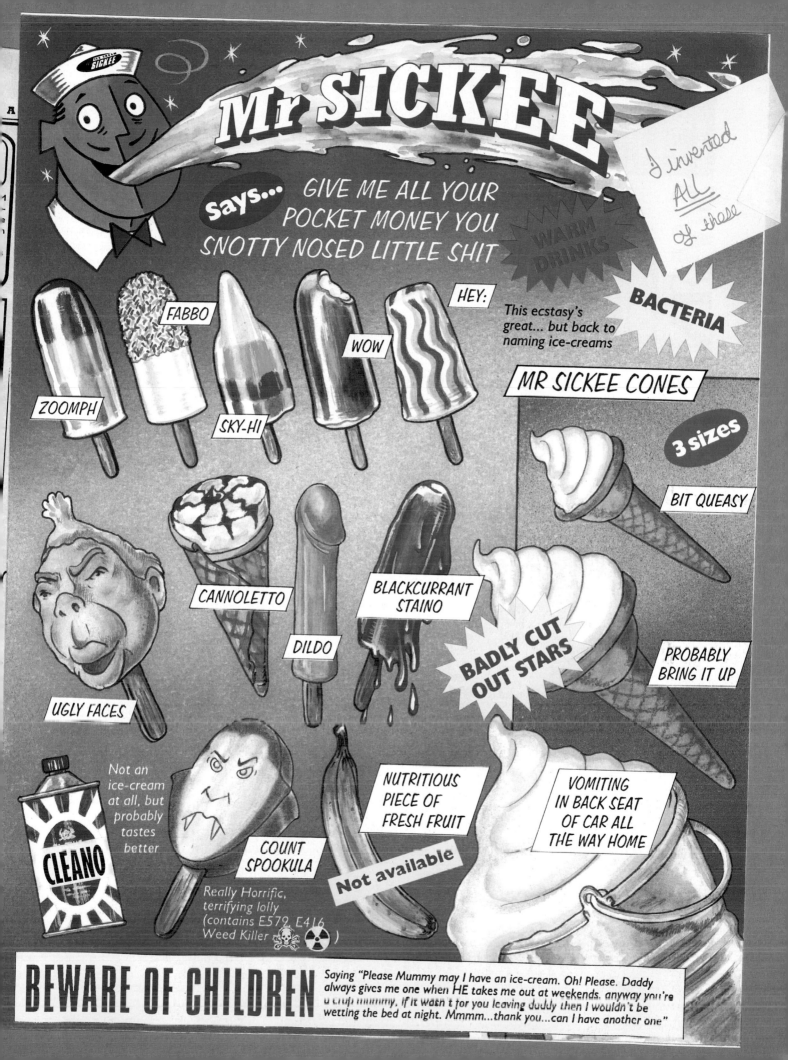

# THE GRANTHAM NEWS

Formerly The Grantham Bugle, previous to that The Grantham Chronicle, before that pieces of blank paper, earlier still a roll in a paper mill, proir to that a nice tree in a forest...oh shut up

October 1959     Published: Thursdays, providing we can borrow a typewriter     Price 3d in old money

## Local girl wins seat in Parliament

L OCAL GIRL MRS MARGOT Thatcher was today elected to Parliament as a first time MP

Mrs Thatcher nee Roberts is the first Grantham Girl to pull herself up from her humble provincial background and break into the posh world of politics, but it hasn't changed her. She still speaks fondly of her childhood as a Lincolnshire shopkeeper's daughter.

"I say, I think you must have the wrong Mrs Thatcher don't you know old chap tally-ho and toodle pip" she said in a rather high pitched impression of a posh person.

Our reporter reminded her of the days when she scrimped and saved a few pennies to get into the Young Conservatives Dance – 'No, no you must be mistaken old bean" she went on "I'm really very refined and cultured and went to Rodean and a Swiss Finishing School – oh bugger all the brown sauce has gone and squirted out of me chip butty.'

Meanwhile ex-neighbours of the new MP remember the days she worked behind the counter of her father's shop.

"She was always a very thrifty young girl", said Edna Bewdley from Rommel Road, "My husband asked for something on tick once. After that we could never have children." Mr Bewdley added: "I remember asking for a bottle milk stout which cost 2/6. When I said it was for medicinal purposes she put it up to three quid."

Though Margot has been elected for a seat in London she says she's still got plans for Grantham. 'Never going there ever again' she pledged.

### Man swindles local bank of Millions

A man swindled his local bank of millions of pounds in the opening chapter of a new detective novel that I started reading yesterday.

### International jewel thief at large

The story, about an international jewel thief at large, is set in the glamourous world of Monte Carlo, and does not have a Grantham connection.

### Grantham connection

But in a dramatic local twist

### Local man involved

A local bookseller today confirmed that if anyone wanted a copy of the book he would try and get it.

**OTHER NEWS IN BRIEF**

### Grantham could hold next Olympics

Grantham could hold the next Olympics, if it was bigger, and probably, not in Britain, and not called Grantham, it was claimed today.

### Quaint Old Motor Cars Ltd

STOCKISTS of RILEY, SUNBEAM, SWOLSEY, SINGER, HILLMAN, HUMBER and all those other British cars that won't be around in twenty years time because the Japs will have taken over.

ALL MAKES SERVICED by our qualified team of mechanics with grubby hands and humble ways who doff their caps and treat you like Royalty and say things like "I dare say we can take a look Sir. I'll see if the missus can't make you a cup of tea" and that's something else you won't get in the future.

Petrol 1-star, no-star from a proper pump

## Grantham to twin with Newark

I N A SENSATIONAL move today, it was announced that Grantham plans to open up discussions with local rival Newark with a view to the two towns twinning. "It makes much more sense than twinning with somewhere foreign that we don't know," said Major Reginald Bewdley, chairman of the Grantham Twinning Committee.

"We know Newark well and it has some good shops. And you can get there on the bus. Unlike somewhere in France that takes forever to get to and has funny food, and they don't speak the language and like the things we do – and let us down in the war, the damned swine".

## Sports report

### Grantham v Newark

THE MATCH was helñ in black and white with both teams wearing baggy shorts and their shirts tucked in. The Grantham skipper scored first but there was none of this hugging and kissing nonsense you'll probably get in the future – it was just a firm handshake and a manly pat on the back. The match was well-attended by lots of men in cloth caps and woolly scarves. The kids were passed down to the front and there was no crowd violence or bad language.

## Editor of Grantham News is bored

"I'M SO FUCKING bored" the Editor of this paper announced today, staring out of the office window at the dull, dirty, soulless little high street. "The same provincial, small-minded, petty, wingeing stories week after week, I can't stand it, they're such horrible narrow-minded little bigots", he told the room.

"Graaaaaaghhhhh! he added, flinging his typewriter through the office window.dowxxfjfivbg;/JRh;vh;ifdoujcxkjknv

## Residents fight to change by-pass route

ANGRY LOCAL RESIDENTS barracked councillors this week at a stormy meeting about the controversial Grantham By-Pass, and accused the Council of betraying them over the new road.

Mrs Edna Bewdley said: "We've fought hard for this by-pass and now they're telling us it won't be going through the town – it's being built five miles away where we can't even see it."

Major Reginald Bewdley, chairman of the By-Pass Campaign, said: "Several times an hour a huge lorry rumbles past my house, making it shake to its foundations. It makes the day more interesting. Now the Council kill-joys want to stop it."

He proposes a new by-pass to by-pass the other by-pass and re-route traffic back through the town.

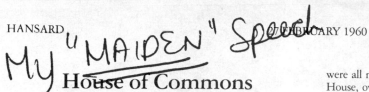

# House of Commons

*February 27th 1960*

*The house met at half past Two o' the clock*

## PRAYERS

{MR SPEAKER *in the chair*}

*A runnin' round o' the woolsack*
*A jiggle o'er black rod's mace*
*Ye other pointless archaic custom*

## PRIVATE BUSINESS

THE BENSON PATENT CANDLE CO LTD BILL

LONDON REGIONAL TRANSPORT (BE BETTER) BILL

THE FOR GOD'S SAKE CAN WE GET ON WITH IT BILL

## DEBATE ON FISHERIES AND CUSTOMS (NOT VERY INTERESTING) BILL *(Second Reading)*

**Mr Harold Macmillan (Stockton-on-Tees):** Mr Speaker! You've never had it so good!

**Mr Hugh Gaitskill (Poor bit north):** How can this Government be so self-satisfied when unemployment is up to nearly five hundred people, a packet of Strand cigarettes costs anything up to 1d and our youngsters are being led astray by the dangerous and subversive modern fashion called 'skiffle' music??

**Honourable Members:** Hear hear!

**Mr Macmillan:** You've never had it so good...

**Honourable Members:** *(Groans)*

**Mr William Gladstone (Old Sarum):** I would like to add... erghh! *(Honourable member dies)*

**Mr Speaker:** I call on... er, the Honourable Member for Finchley!

**Mrs Margaret Thatcher (Finchley):** Me? Ooh er gosh!

**Mr Speaker:** Yes, you! go on!

**Honourable Members:** I say isn't that a girlie?/Gosh, she's got breasts/etc

**Mr Speaker:** C'mon m'girl!

**Mrs Thatcher:** Um, Mr Speaker! Er... um, sorry, I... er, I – I should like to – er – I've gone blank. Where are my notes?

**Mr Edward Heath (Old Bexley and Sidcup):** Get on with it!

**Mrs Thatcher:** *(Shuffles papers)* I would like to start by thanking the previous member for Finchley for dying – I mean, all the hard work he's put into my constituency – his constituency... er, furthermore, I – I mean look, why don't I do my shadow puppets? This is a butterfly...

**Honourable Members:** *(Laughter and derision)*

**Mrs Thatcher:** *(Bursts into tears)* Boo-hoo!

**Mr Speaker:** Something wrong my dear?

**Mrs Thatcher:** It's just – this is such an important moment for me, and I've practiced so long in the mirror, and now it's all going terribly, terribly wrong!

**Mr Speaker:** *(Patting Honourable Member's hand)* There, there, we

were all new once y'know. Why, I remember *my* first time in the House, over forty years ago... *(Mr Speaker relates two hour anecdote about meeting Lloyd George)... and that was how it all happened. So – there's no need for *you* to be sad!

**Mrs Thatcher:** Zzzzzz...

**Mr Speaker:** Margaret!

**Mrs Thatcher:** What? Oh yes, thank you...

**Mr Speaker:** Here, dry your eyes. Pretty little thing aren't you?

**Mrs Thatcher:** Thank you sir.

**Mr Speaker:** What are you doing for dinner tonight?

**Mr Heath:** Ooh! Don't let *him* get his claws in you, dear. It's not his real hair you know.

**Dr David Owen (Devonport):** Can I just say I'll *always* be a member of the Socialist Worker's Party?

**Mr Macmillan:** You've never had it so good!

**Mr Speaker:** Look, can we get on with things! *(Voice softens)* Margaret - do carry on.

**Mrs Thatcher:** Thank you. Where was I? Well -

**Mr John Profumo (Legover South):** Will the Honourable Member give way?

**Mrs Thatcher:** Er – well if I must...

**Mr John Profumo:** I just want to say that everyone's invited to a party at Cliveden this weekend – loads of skirt, and there's a charming Russian chap with a tape recorder. Bring a bottle and a bird.

**Honourable Members:** *(cheering, lustful gestures etc)*

**Mr Speaker:** Order! Order!

**Mr Gaitskill:** Is the Prime Minister aware that the Channel Tunnel is over a *week* overdue??

**Honourable Members:** *(Jeers)*

**Mrs Thatcher:** Shut up!!

*Stunned Honourable Members fall silent*

**Mrs Thatcher:** That's it! I've had *enough* of playing the poor little new girl!

**Mr Speaker:** But

**Mrs Thatcher:** Shut up you old goat!

**Honourable Members:** Gasp! She's just like Nanny! *(Shiver of pleasure runs down spines)*

**Mrs Thatcher:** I may be new round here, but one day I'll be leader of this party! I'll win three elections and end up being Britain's longest-serving Prime Minister this century! I'll go on and on and on! Rejoice! Rejoice! *(Lashes benches with whip. Honourable Members recoil in fear)*

**Mr John Stonehouse (Frinton Beach East):** Oh sure! And I'll leave all my clothes on the beach and pretend to have topped myself!

**Mr Macmillan:** You've never had it so good! *(Drops ear trumpet)* Oh dear. I think I've been a messy boy.

**Nurse (St Thomas', Geriatric):** There there, it's not your fault dear.

**That Was The Week That Was (Oxbridge Central):** I put it to the Prime Minister that he is not... very good!

**Honourable Members:** *(Gasps)*

**Mr David Frost (Footlights South):** And furthermore... he is quite old!

**Honourable Members:** *(Astonished gasps. Government collapses ushering in brief era of Labour rule which is apparently responsible for all problems ever after)*

# Snow White and the Seven Dwarf

**O**nce upon a time there were seven dwarfs although four dwarfs would have been economically viable.

One day they returned home from the oversubsidised mine after a cushy seventeen-hour shift underground, to find a beautiful young woman in their cottage.

"Have you come to cook and clean for us?" they asked excitedly.

"No, I've come to deliver your redundancy notices" explained Snow White.

"Hurrah!" they exclaimed. "At last someone is prepared to take tough but necessary decisions." And they danced with glee as she boarded up their little cottage.

"But what will we do now?" said Dole

"There's plenty of work for a skilled miner – delivering pizzas, driving mini-ca selling dusters door-to-door."

And so they all lived happily ever afte But then this *is* a fairy tale.

HI HO, HI HO – IT'S ON THE DOLE WE GO!

# BENDOVER
## PUBLIC SCHOOL FOR BOYS

**Y**ou can always spot a Bendover man – he's the one in the restaurant throwing bread rolls. Here at Bendover we pride ourselves on producing the sort of chaps who have made Britain what it is today.

Bendover old-boys include such famous figures as that City exec who went to jail, the one who cocked up that jewellery scam, and the one who did his Nanny in and buggered off.

But we don't accept just anyone at Bendover. We have a rigourous entrance exam – finding the door marked 'Entrance'.

## Academic Curriculum

Bendover offers its boys the chance to excell at many subjects including:

**English**
**History**
**Latin**
**Masturbation**
**Bullying**
**Blushing in front of girls**
**Laughing with your upper teeth sticking out**

## Extra-Mural activities

Bendover feels young boys should be give every opportunity to prepare for adult life. Hence we offer special evening and weekend classes in talking too loudly in wine-bars, crashing sports cars and credit card fraud.

### Scholarships

Bendover School has always sought to attract boys who... well, attract boys, Each year we try to provide scholarships for boys from poorer families who seem exceptionally homosexually gifted. If you think you may be eligible then feel free to come into the office and pick up a form, or the Greek master, whichever you prefer.

### Fees

Due to careful financial planning, we are able to set our fees at a level which is slightly more than you can afford.

You may choose your method of payment; the most popular is to struggle along for a couple of terms until you go bankrupt, forcing you to enrol your son in the local secondary modern where he will have the shit beaten out of him for ever after.

### A fine start

As caring parents, you will want your child to have the very best start in life possible. That aside, we hope you will consider Bendover for your offspring.

## THE WEE BOOK OF CHRISTIAN NAMES

**Caitlin** An Irish Gaelic version of Catherine. A good name if you wish your daughter to be delayed for three hours by security staff at Heathrow.

**Camilla** Meaning 'horsey Sloane', platonic companion of Royal Prince and not at all his 'bit on the side', honest.

**Carol** From the old French, meaning 'second rate journalist who used to appear on boorish Radio 4 show and fail to realise that everyone was laughing at her.'

**Cassandra** Meaning 'beautiful but unobtainable posh girl, school lacrosse captain, brilliant sister and winner of countless gymkhanas. Haver of a very nice life, thank you.'

**Barry** From the Saxon, meaning 'always in the wrong place.'

**Ceinwen/Ceinwyn** Ancient Celt name meaning 'usually spelt wrong.'

**Charlene** Meaning 'daughter of very poor parents who are both on the dole and live on the sixteenth floor of a council flat where she will grow up frustrated and deprived and generally have a much worse life than Cassandra.'

**Corinne** See 'Charlene.'

**C'n'ere!** The name Charlene and Corinne think they've got.

**Cosmo** Meaning parents thought they were trendy in the seventies but were actually very short-sighted and have ended up naming their child after a second-rate women's magazine.

**Crap-me-pants-cabbage-breath** An uncommon name meaning 'unplanned baby very much resented by parents who want to give it a hard time at school after all the trouble it's caused them.'

# Woman about the house

An idea for a hilarious sitcom based on my life in the 70's
BY M. THATCHER

MAGGIE THATCHER Me
TED HEATH Ted Heath
WILLIE WHITELAW Arthur Mullard
JIM PRIOR June Whitfield
GEOFFREY HOWE A Pile of Bat's Droppings
A WORKING CLASS CHAPPIE A Posh Actor Who Can't Do The Accent

It's the Seventies. The interior of a shabby bachelor flat, aka 10 Downing Street. It has been badly run by the present occupant, Ted, a feckless namby-pamby who let it go to rack and ruin. He is seated at the breakfast table with his gormless flatmates, Willie, Geoffrey and Jim. They are surrounded by several years' washing up...

TED: Never mind all this housework – I'm going yachting tomorrow. Has anyone seen my flares?
WILLIE: Yes – they're on the bottom of your trousers!
TED: Ooh! For heaven's sake Willie! Not those sort of flares – I meant those rocket things you use to signal distress at sea!

The studio audience laugh at this brilliant play on words.

JIM: Well I would have thought those flares you're wearing are perfect – they're so bright, you could see them fifty miles away!

The studio audience clutch their sides. They are in stitches.

TED: Oh, by the way everyone, there's something I've been meaning to tell you. It's to do with the fact that we're all boys together...

His flatmates look embarrassed, fidget, cough, cross their legs etc.

TED: ...I think it's high time we had a woman about the house.
GEOFFREY: A woman?!
WILLIE: But she'll ruin everything!
TED: Nonsense – that's my job!

The audience applauds at the truth of this observation.

GEOFFREY: Well I'm not going to stand for it. If there's a woman in the house, we'll have to change our underpants and hoover the mould off the bread and put up with soppy flowers and all sorts of girlie things.
MAGGIE: (Off) Yoo hoo boys! How do you like my new tank top?

Maggie enters wearing a 'tank top'. It is the top half of a tank! The studio audience applauds wildly.

MAGGIE: (Modestly waits for the cheers to subside) They don't call me the Iron Lady for nothing!
TED: Oh no? Well you can start by doing some ironing then!

He hands her an iron. She deliberately drops it on his foot. Audience cheer.

TED: Ooh! Ow! My foot! Ooh ouch ooh!

He hops around unconvincingly

JIM: Mark my words, this will end in trouble, or I've never watched an episode of Terry and June.
TED: (Nursing his foot) Don't worry Jim, I'm in charge. She's only here to clean and cook for us...

(The passing of time is denoted by a whimsical musical link...). Someone is cooking at the stove in a pinafore... But it's not Maggie – it's Ted!

MAGGIE: (Off) Hurry up with my dinner! I've been waiting longer than a passenger in On The Buses!
TED: Er... just coming dear. (To himself) Oh no! Dinner's going to be ruined – and all because somebody's stolen the milk!

Maggie is in the living room, hiding some milk bottles (the good old fashioned ones and not these silly dumpy ones we have now)...

MAGGIE: (Winks to camera) They don't call me milk snatcher for nothing.

Ted enters carrying plates of food. The dinner is burnt to a frazzle.

TED: Dinner!
JIM: Dinner? Looks more like a lump of coal!
MAGGIE: Don't say that to Ted – he'll probably give it a massive subsidy.

Audience nod in earnest agreement at this pertinent satirical point.

MAGGIE: Really! This house is a complete shambles! In fact it's high time someone else took over, and I wouldn't be at all surprised if someone called at the door to emphasise the point...

The doorbell rings. A working class chappie is standing there with one of those clipboard things that working class people have.

WORKING CLASS CHAPPIE: Begging yer pardon guvnor, but unless you pays us more money, me and the lads has come to cut your electricity off and hold the country to ransom.
TED: (Quaking in his shoes) Yes, yes, whatever you say! I'll give you anything you like!
WORKING CLASS CHAPPIE: And seein' as how you're such a bloomin' pushover – we're going on a three-day week!
MAGGIE: Well that's two more than you usually work!

The studio audience rise to their feet as one, whoop, cheer, throw flowers, sing Land of Hope and Glory and re-discover their National Pride as the Working Class Chappie cringes before her.

TED: Now look here Maggie! I'm fed up with you interfering! It's high time we had a house meeting...

(The passing of time is denoted by a whimsical musical link...)

TED: ... Hands up if you agree there can only be one head of this household.

Everyone's hand goes up.

TED: So that's settled then – off you go Maggie!
WILLIE: Her?
JIM: No – we want rid of you!
TED: But... but... I... Oh no! (Does his soon-to-be-famous 'oh no' catchphrase)

Cheers, applause, credits and a signature tune by Ronnie Hazelhurst.

THE END

*ITV*
Sitcom Department

Plywood House
Sofa Street
Hamshire OLD HAT

Dear

Thank you for submitting your situat[ion]

I have:- Lost it ☐ Kept it in a drawer for months ☐ Kept it in a drawer for months and then lost it ☐ Finally got round to reading the bloody thing ☑
I regret that it is unsuitable for transmission on ITV as it contains a joke.

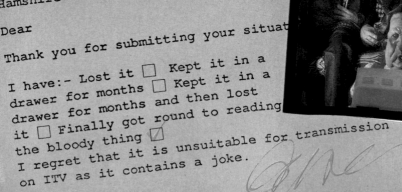

I'm the LEADER, I'm the LEADER.
I'm the leader of the gang I AM.

**QUALITY CONTROL**
Red Eye – Your subject-matter has been over-exposed to alcohol. Make her drink a lot of water and get a good night's sleep.
LIFT & PEEL HERE
**ADVICE LABEL**

**QUALITY CONTROL**
Bad choice of cabinet – You have ill-chosen your cabinet. Suggest you watch out that the one on the left doesn't make a speech on Europe that leads to a challenge to your leadership by the one on your right ensuring your ignominious downfall.
LIFT & PEEL HERE
**ADVICE LABEL**

---

IDEAS FOR VICTORY SPEECH
(to be spoken movingly on steps of Downing St.)

I would like to quote St Francis of Assisi:
"Lets all be really nice to the animals"
~~Lets all be really nice to the animals~~    Too Woolley

See these election promises? (TEAR UP MANIFESTO) Ha ha you suckers!
save for later

I would like to quote St Francis of Assisi:
Where there is discord, may we bring harmony.
Where there is error, may we bring truth.
Where there is doubt, may we bring faith.
Where there is despair, may we bring hope.
Where there are prescription charges of 10p,
may we put them up to over four quid.
        Perfect !!! But perhaps lose the last bit.

Yeeeeeeeeeeaaaaaaaahhh! Yeeeeeeeaaaaahhh!
Woooh! Woooh! Woooh! Wooooh! I wooooooooonnnn!
Woah! I fucking won! Oi oi Jim! See this finger? See this finger, right? Sit on that! Sit and spin! Youuuuuuuuu're shit! Ha!
Yeeeeeeeeaaaaaaahhh! Woooooooooooaahhhhhh!

Ha ha, you foolish terrans are so puny. You bend before my inflexible will. I will conquer your human planet and rape its feeble resources. Your world will soon be a charred husk. Perish, humans! Oh perish, I am the master now!
        Whoops !!!

save for private reception

---

**QUALITY CONTROL**
You have taken a perfectly decent photograph but we've stuck on one of these bloody stickers anyway, and when you try to pull it off half the picture will come away and the other half will leave a gluey smear which will get all grubby, but putting stickers on your photos is the only thing which brightens up the dreary world of processing endless snaps of other people's office parties, skiing trips and new born babies and briefly gives a small sense of power to the spotty oik in the nylon shirt who gets to stick them on.
LIFT & PEEL HERE
**ADVICE LABEL**

# Michael & Angelo
## *Interior Designers to the Beautiful People*

**INVOICE**

Job No: 10/0 CRINGE/GHASTL 1E

To: *Mrs. H. Thatcher, 10 Downing St. London.*

For: *Work to her exact instructions*

A nice little flat
in Hampstead,
London,
NW1H 0MO

**Hall and Stairs:** Scrape off 'silly picture' by Rubens from ceiling, glue up polystyrene tiles. Re-paper through out with floral anaglypta wallpaper (Do-It-All receipt attached). Knock down classical pillars which are 'a bit old'. Carpet through out with thick fluffy white nylon stuff (bulk order from Lucky Gonk toy factory).

**Drawing Room:** Rip out Victorian fireplace, replace with gas-fired heater with real plastic log effect. Re-upholster Regency style chaise-longue in pink draylon, with lime green fluffy scatter cushions. Put mahogany table and Chippendale chair set on skip; replace with six-seater zebra pattern leather corner suite, matching pouffée. Remove Bechstein grand piano. Install Yamaha electronic home organ (with rhythm machine). Also, 'Barrier Reef' theme cocktail bar, tropical fish-tank.

**Library:** Replace Queen Anne walnut veneer writing desk with self-assembly chipboard 'work station' from Officeland. Burn all those tatty old 'books' – replenish shelves with complete Dick Francis collection, set of the 'Summer Wine' videos, and the odd Jeffrey Archer novel!

**Exterior:** Stone cladding front and back. Fit mock wagon wheels. Remove brass door knocker, install 'National Anthem' chime door-bell.

**nb:** Unthinkable, heritagewise

---

---

## T – TWITS, UPPER CLASS

**TAYLOR, Elizabeth.** born: Mind your own business. *Married:* Not enough. *Address:* Betty Ford Clinic. *Recreation:* Yoursh my besht pal, room on form. gimme another drinksh hic...

**THATCHER, Rt. Hon Mrs. Margaret (Hilda)** M.P. Finchley since 1959; Prime Minister and First Lord of the Treasury since 1979; *b* 13 Oct 1925 *d* of late Alfred Roberts, Grantham Lincs. Formidable but unpopular political leader renowned for her interventionist approach into all aspects of the media and publishing, ooh hang on there's someone at the door – oh Prime Minister, this is a pleasant surprise and who might these large gentlemen with the bent noses be – oww, leggo my arm, now look here, you can't barge in here and tell me what to – een, my hair sffkkg stop banging sffkyyykkk my head on the typewriter sfxxxbbvh-9ui vbikvfih what are you doing with those crocodile clips n ho

**THATCHER, Rt. Hon Mrs. Margaret (Hilda)** M.P. Finchley since 1959, Prime Minister and First Lord of the Treasury since 1979; *b* 13 Oct 1925 *d* of late Alfred Roberts, Grantham Lincs, and my goodness what a wonderful lady she is, yes indeedy, inventor of the wheel and sliced bread, discovered penicillin, scored that trick in World Cup final 1966, writer of Dad's Army and first person on Moon, yet still finds time to be a loving wife and mother, all hail Mother, she should really be Queen oh yes definitely, and it's perfectly reasonable that she should've wired my testicles to this car battery.

**THOMPSON-...** well, doesn't want to be either.

*Publisher's note:* Reverend Thompson-Smythe has just been found dead at desk downwards

**THOMPSON-SMYTHE, Reverend, George, (Anthony).** *Married* to ... beside smoking revolver.

**THOMPSON-SMYTHE, Reverend, George, (Anthony).** *Member:* Lay Committee on Church Affairs, (chairman 1988-9) *Founder:* Society of Educational Trusts, Alderman 1967-7. *Governor:* Bridewell Royal Hospital 1974. *Trustee:* National Flood and Tempest Distress Fund 1977, Church Commissioner for England, 1983-9. *Member:* National Committee of Good Works, 1984-... George mate, when are you going to start enjoying life, go on, take a night off, go out and get pissed, have a curry, get into a fight – I mean have you ever thought what you're doing when you're at all these meetings? Well you know that succession of young gardeners you've had, she let's them tie her to the bed and then they cover her in baby oil and – anyway, *I've* had her, we all have, I only want round there to get your form.... We did it on *your* bed Reverend, she lay back and said take me you giant steam hammer.' She told me you were dead from the waist

**THWISTLETON, Brigadier Sir Charles (Farquarhar).** Head of anti-terrorist operations N. Ireland 1984-89. Obvious soft target for IRA but here's his address anyway The Old Mill, Cookham Berkshire. *Club:* The Temple Golf Club. He usually leaves his Jaguar in the driveway. Tuesdays are probably best, only use the side gate he can't see you from the bar.

**TONY,** the bloke in my off licence. *b* 27th March 1962. *Educated:* Bracknell Comprehensive, left early after letting off banger in assembly, to concentrate on poorly paid building work. *m* Sharon (nee Norris) May 1989. : Darren (Elvis) *b* June 1989. Unemployed 1979-88. *Recreation:* karaoke, mending Cortina, walking round with rottweiler. Not actually famous at all, but I promised to put him in if he let me have a bottle of Mouton-Cadet, look I was on my way to a dinner party and I'd forgotten my cheque book, what would you have done?

THE CORRESPONDENCE OF A VERY IMPORTANT LADY – Just an average day's post-bag for the PRIME MINISTER of BRITAIN!

To: M. Thatcher
10, Downing St. London, England

We have in our possession:
. One public school twit (with car)
Please claim within next 7 days
    or it will be sold by auction

- - - - - - - - - - - - - - - - - - - - - -

# THE COUNCIL OF BRITISH CHURCHES

Dear Mrs Thatcher,

As the religious leaders of all the main Christian denominations in Britain we are writing to you to express concern at the social cost of some of your policies.

Yes, you may have ignored mass demonstrations, year-long strikes and cabinet resignations, but we thought a letter from a few bishops might really be the thing to make you reverse everything you've done so far.

I know it's ridiculous isn't it? I said it was a stupid idea at our meeting, but they thought it would make the Church look a bit upbeat and concerned about current affairs, so muggins here got lumbered with the job of putting pen to paper.

So how about it? How about stripping the rich of their ill gotten gains and spending it on a massive job creation programme, reviving the health service and giving me a new church roof? I know you won't have bothered reading this far so I can write what I want. I'm gay. I'm homosexual. I've wanted to tell the whole world for so long but I daren't. Nobody knows except the verger. I wish I could just retire with him to a little village in Suffolk, but of course it would break Marjorie's heart. She thinks I go to choir practice on Tuesday evenings.

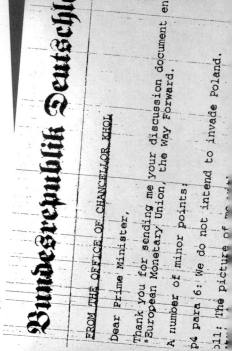

FROM THE OFFICE OF CHANCELLOR KHOL

Dear Prime Minister,

Thank you for sending me your discussion document ent "European Monetary Union, the Way Forward.

A number of minor points:

p4 para 6: We do not intend to invade Poland.

p11: The picture of me with

---

## THE GRAND
★★★★★
BRIGHTON

Dear Mrs Thatcher
        Thank you for your letter.
We feel that under the circumstances your request for a refund is a reasonable one.
        However, it has been brought to my attention that two towels and an ashtray are still missing and we were wondering if you may have accidentally

---

# Hezbollah

'Bringing Ji'Had to you'

Remains of Floor Nine,
Burnt out Tower block
Crater Ave, off Rubble Drive
Knock twice and ask for Abdul.

Dear Mrs Thatcher,

Thank you for your letter of the first inst.; however, we regret that we are unable to take hostages on request, and therefore are returning your list.

Yours fundamentally,

Abdul Al Mad-mahn,

Head of All-out War against the Infidel

Enclos.

# Labour
**Putting lots of 'ing' words in our slogans**

## A personal invitation to join the Labour Party from Neil Kinnock MP

To Mrs. M Thatcher
Position Leader of the Conservative Party

Dear Mrs. M Thatcher

The Labour Party has in the past been criticised for inefficiency and money-wasting. But we believe those days are behind us and this personalised mailshot to you, Mrs Thatcher is the sort of sophisticated target mailing we can now achieve. Our brand new and rather expensive computer has told us that you, Mrs Thatcher are the sort of Labour Party supporter that we should be reaching out to. So please give whatever you can to get rid of Mrs Thatcher, Mrs Thatcher.

☐ £5 could pay for a badly aimed leaflet like this one.

☐ £50 could pay for a lunch for some dreadful city yuppies who are thinking 'Why are this lot trying to butter us up – we're never going to vote for them.'

☐ £75 could pay for a flashy silk tie for Peter Mandelson.

☐ £100 could go towards winning the next election, although obviously, when we lose it, you won't get a refund.

☐ £150 is frankly more than you're ever going to give, so I don't know why we put this box here.

### By joining the Labour Party you will be able to:

● Go to meetings with a bunch of bearded pedants and embittered loners in anoraks.

● Have an MI5 file opened in your name.

● Pass lots of embarrassing left-wing resolutions which we ignore after the conference.

*P.S. I hope you will give whatever you can. These phoney post scripts in different coloured ink cost money you know!* *Neil Kinnock*

**Please return this form with your donation to:**
Neil Kinnock, (he will be opening the envelope, honest)
The Labour Party, Grotty House, Nowhere Near,
Westminster, London SE1

You do not have to affix a stamp, but if you don't the letter won't get here.

# Labour

---

You are cordially invited to a

# GARDEN PARTY

at 4.00pm on 21st July

in the presence of Her Majesty the Queen,
His Royal Highness Prince Philip Duke of Edinburgh, Her Royal Highne...
Princess Margaret – oohh no! Do we have to invite that woman?
Yes we do, she is one's sister after all. Oh well, lock up the bloody gin then.
Philip! Now where was I... Her Royal Highness Princess Michael of Kent –
oh no, not old 'Princess Pushy'! Why is she coming? Well, she came last year.
Yes, no one invited her though. And then there's that young man with a Mohican
hair cut and a 4-pack of lager who always comes.
Which side of the family's he from? I don't know, says he knows 'Dave'?

RSVP: BUCKINGHAM PALACE
1, PALL MALL, LONDON W1 (Top bell)

*Vicars & twts*

DRESS: ~~BLACK TIE~~

---

# VISION REPAIR
**109b, Victoria St. London SW1 ☎ 071 973 6372**

Dear Mrs. Thatcher

We have located the fault in your TV set / video recorder

Problem ...... Set broke down during

...... "Death on the Rock"

Fault ...... Large axe through screen.

# THE MAKING OF A STATESWOMAN

In 1975 Conservative Central Office got a shock when they did a survey of people's reaction to their new leader. 60% said they found the pictures totally repellent. The other 40% of surveys were too covered in sick to be legible. Wayne Kerr, Creative Director of Hugh, Kerr, Creative Director of Hugh, Pugh, Barney McGrew, Cuthbert, Dibble and Grub takes up the story

**Stage four:** Almost perfect – the teeth are straight, the cheekbones and hair soft and attractive. Conservative Central Office, however, thought there was possibly one are too many. At this stage, they made the

**Stage one:** This was the problem that confronted us in 1975. In image maker's terms, she was what was known in the trade as a 'hectoring old cow'. After analysing hundreds of hours of news footage and TV interviews, paying particular attention to her personal style, relationship with the camera, the way she moved and so on – we were able to recommend a solution: major plastic surgery.

**Stage two:** Our first attempt: not a success – maybe we shouldn't have tried to bring out the PM's natural personality.

**Stage three:** We liked this look a lot; it's dramatic, it's engaging, but Conservative Central office felt it was "a bit lizardy."

**Stage five:** This proved not to be a good idea. Too many different opinions. In the end we told the plastic surgeon to come up with something himself.

**Stage six:** Great! For me, this was the one – but Central Office had a feeling that the look had been used before.

**At this point HPBMCD&G lost the account, whilst Margaret Thatcher goes on to record the smash hit 'I got you babe'.**

COMPLAIGN 24 JULY 1990

*A wonderful marriage (or so we thought)*

## 1

### ARCHBISHOP'S WELCOMING ADDRESS

**ARCHBISHOP:** Hello everybody! Well, it's lovely to see you all here for this most joyous of national occasions. Now before we start, there's to be no confetti either inside or outside the church – it's a lot of extra work for old Mrs Harris, I mean she has the flower arranging and Westminster Abbey to do as well you know. By the way, contributions for the new roof are always welcome – we managed to raise £61 at last Saturday's jumble sale! Only another £5 million to go...

**CONGREGATION:** Oh get on with it!

**ARCHBISHOP:** Sorry. Let us begin with a modern gospel hymn! Hallelujah!

### MODERN GOSPEL SONG
#### SUNG BY MR CLIFF RICHARD
*(Tambourines will be provided)*

**CLIFF:** Wo-ah luvvin' Jesus is still cool!
It doesn't make you square!
Just cos we wear aran jumpers
and drink lots of cocoa, yeah!
We like to clap our hands wo yeah!
and be happy all the time
and not drink, or smoke, or have a shag
or have fun of any kind

*Andrew and bridesmaid*

*Order of Service*

The wedding of His Royal Earness Prince Charles
AND
Some Suitable Royal Baby Provider
AT ST PAUL'S CATHEDRAL
VICAR: ARCHBISHOP OF CANTERBURY, ROBERT 'BOB' RUNCIE
TIME: 2:30PM PROMPT,
WITH A FEW WANDERING IN LATE FROM THE PUB

*make my usual stylish entrance*

## 2

**CHORUS:** Oh Hallelujah! Jesus! It's a really happenin' scene
To spend your free time saying 'Jesus' and bashing tambourines
Wo! Jesus! Hallejulah! (etc)
Hallejulah! Jesus!

*(Continues for two hours. Short interval as congregation are treated for hand sores and wrist sprain)*

### PRAYER LED BY THE ARCHBISHOP

Archbishop: Oh Lord God... for those of us who believe there is a God. I mean, I don't want to cause any divisions – ours is a broad Church, and there's room for a more spiritual – as opposed to literal – interpretation of the word 'God'. Of course, I don't want to give the impression I'm sitting on the fence over this one, but it's very difficult...

*Congregation spring awake at sound of organ playing first few bars of...*

### HYMN NUMBER 413

**CONGREGATION:** Lord of all hope-fullness, Lord of all light!
Oh mumble, mumble-mumble, don't really know the tune
Oh God I'm so bored with this long, long service
Hope that the food is good
at the reception later on

Oh Lord there's yet another verse, let's hope it's the last
It's so cold in this bloody place, wish I'd worn that other shirt
and take out that bloody baby, that's screaming at the back
and the bloke with that camcorder is really getting on my tits

*The groom and ~~best man~~.*

## 3

*Oh... not more of this tedious hymn! Oh God I'm so bored!
I'm desperate for a piss now please please let it stop
Oh hang on I think we're finishing, and I know this last bit
So I'll really belt it out and impress everyone
At – the – end – of – the – day*

**RUNCIE:** Well, almost time for the big moment! But first His Royal Highness Prince Edward has insisted – er– volunteered to perform a piece from his university review...
*(Congregation will give barely audible groan)*

*(Edward now dances up the aisle sideways wearing boater and stripey blazer)*

**EDWARD:** *(Sings jauntily)* Oh! There's nothing quite as jolly!
As taking a girl on a punt!
The only thing that's as jolly
Is putting your hand in – the water
*(Congregation will now cough embarrassedly)*

**EDWARD:** Errr, that's odd! That line got a belter of a laugh at the Variety Michaelmas Ball – oh well!
There's nothing quite as jolly!
As having a hamper of tuck –

**QUEEN:** *(Rising)* That's enough, Edward!
**EDWARD:** Oh Mumsy! *(leaves sulking)*

### WEDDING MARCH

*(Very long Pause. Worried murmurs from Congregation. Scuffle outside Church doors. Bride is dragged in by Royal Bodyguards)*

**ARCHBISHOP:** Dearly Beloved! We are gathered together here, in the sight of two billion TV viewers, to join together

← The bride relaxes after the wedding buffet.

As a special treat, → Edward was allowed half a shandy.

# Michael & Angelo

### _Wedding Arrangers to the Beautiful People_
### _'You find a posh virgin — and we'll do the rest'_

**INVOICE No:** V/COST/L1E

| | |
|---|---|
| Hire of St.Paul's Cathedral | £3,000,000 |
| Wedding Bells | £60 extra |
| | |
| Hire of wedding dress | £38,000 |
| Taking in of said dress | £12,352 |
| Letting it out again the same day then | |
| taking it in after lunch | £25,960 |

Use of: Ye Olde Royal Coach, Ye Royal Footmen, Ye Royal Coachmen (fore and aft), Ye Royal stander on side of coach for no apparent reason, Ye Royal head of over-manning on coaches, Ye head of running along behind sweeping up Ye horseshit £239,000

Silly costumes for above (from Carnival Fancy Dress Hire) £89,297

### RECEPTION
Hire of Berkshire suite at the
Schooner Inn, Hendon £12,500
Hire of Gary's Roadshow
Disco £50 + Watney's Party Seven

### BUFFET
Including Special culinary considerations for specific guests as follows:

Prince Charles - no meat

Queen Mother - no fish
Princess Diana - no food
Breznev - Nothing too rich
(such as potatoes or beetroot)
President Reagan - Burgers only
(cut up into small pieces)
Emperor Bokassa - Leaders of
the opposition only £15,000

### PLUS FINGER BUFFET FOR REMAINING 5,000 GUESTS:
| | |
|---|---|
| 30,000 vol-au-vents | £30,000 |
| 5,000 cheesy pineapples | £5,000 |
| One packet of cashew nuts | £10,000 |
| | |
| expensive champagne for Royals | £450,000 |
| Cheap champagne for third world leaders and Princess Margaret | £2.50 |

### ADDITIONAL EXPENSES
| | |
|---|---|
| 10,000 polythene Union Jacks (made in Hong Kong) | £5,000 |
| Hire of 10,000 sycophantic flag waving proles | £10,000,000 |
| 4,000 SAS marksmen stationed on rooftops (in case they don't cheer) | 40,000,000 |

**TOTAL COST (including VAT)** £57,989,768

Minus one bottle of 'Taboo'
returned unopened = £57,989,764.50p

---

**5**

---

_A lively chat about who goes on the stamps_

_After a joyful day, it's time to say goodbye!_

this man and this woman in Holy Unsuitable Matrimony

It is not in anyway meant to be taken in hand lightly, or wantonly, to satisfy men's carnal lusts and appetites like brute beasts that have no understanding _ooh I do like that bit (Mops brow with hankie)_ – no, it is to be done reverently, and not just as a rather clever ruse to knock the recession off the front pages for a few weeks.

If any person here present knows just cause or impediment why these two people should not be manacled together, let them speak now – or wait a few years in the hope of getting even more money out of the papers.

Ahem. Wilt thou Charles George Henry Anastapolopolos

---

England 4 Poland Nil Windsor, have this woman to thy wedded wife, to live together in the Royal estate of Highgrove? Wilt thou ignore her, and not like her very much, and carry on seeing thy previous girlfriends, in sickness and in bucket?

**GROOM:** Errrr, if I must.

**ARCHBISHOP:** Wilt Thou, Diana Jane Blushing Silver-spoon Wallflower Spencer, have this man to be thy wedded husband, to live mainly apart in the Holy estate of matrimony? Wilt thou hate him, and scream at him, and throw thyself down the stairs and into a glass cabinet?

**BRIDE:** I will.

_(Turns to Horsey Sloane who is standing on Charles' other side)_

**ARCHBISHOP:** Wilt thou, Camilla Parker-Bowles, be the 'other woman', and the subject of lots of malicious but highly entertaining gossip?

**HORSEY SLOANE:** Er – okay yarr.

**ARCHBISHOP:** I now pronounce thee man and wife. You may kiss the other bird.

_(The bride and groom will now walk up the aisle, arguing. Organ recital of specially selected pieces by the newly weds)_

### 'THE YING TONG SONG' FROM THE GOON SHOW

### 'YOUNG GUNS GO FOR IT' BY WHAM

_(There will be an interval of ten years, followed by a Royal separation and the collapse of the Monarchy)_

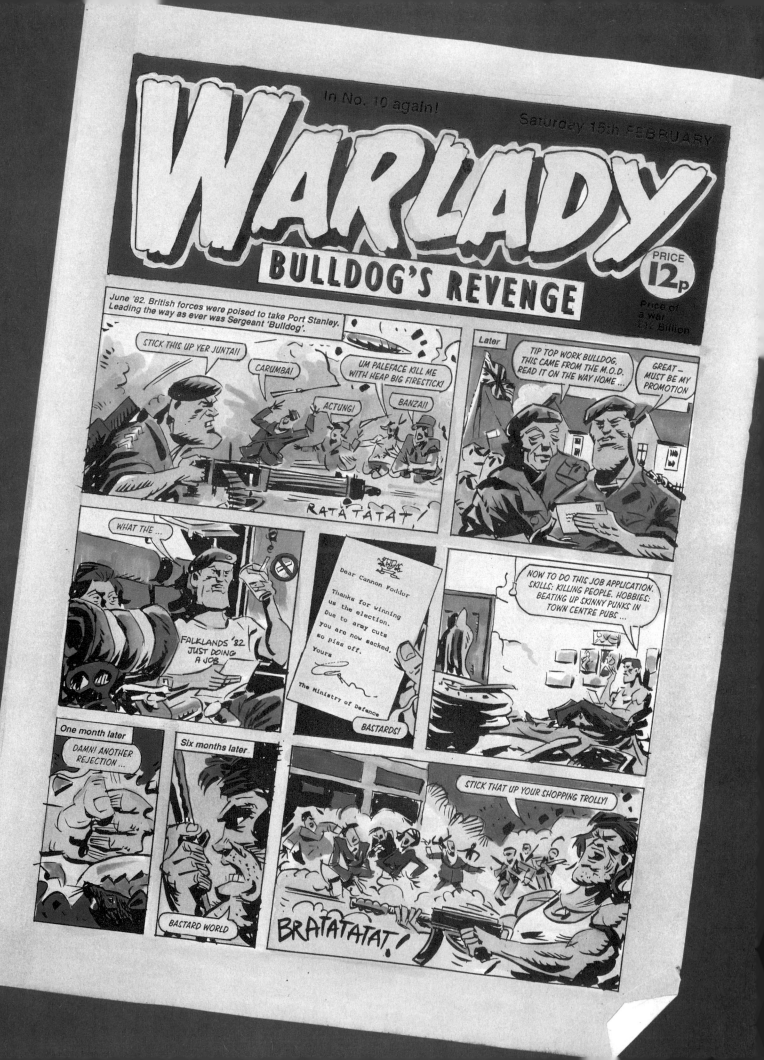

# ROYAL NAVY LOG BOOK Do not remove*

*Er... I think that is on the right — no wait* MODERN BRITISH
*— oh! I see* PLYMOUTH FIGHTING SHIP

VESSEL HMS CONQUEROR PORT PLYMOUTH CLASS MODERN BRITISH FIGHTING SHIP

BUILT 1867 CAPTAIN Rear Admiral Larry "Larry" "Eyepatch" Fitz Nelson

| DATE | POSITION | | COMMENTS |
|------|----------|---|----------|
| | Longitude (No...hang on. It's Latitude isn't it? Which is the one that goes like the equator? Anyway. That one) | The other one | |
| Mar 31st | 25° 34' N $3% 20@ W At home. | | Captain's Log. Stardate 25.6789. Bones, Scotty and Lieutenant Uhuru are marooned on the mining planet Kraal. Suddenly, I have to stop watching Star Trek, as I receive an urgent call from 10 Downing Street. A power-mad dictator is threatening to go to war over some islands in the South Atlantic. As she is my boss I have no choice but to obey her orders. I say goodbye to my wife and tell her that I am bound for the Falkland Islands. She keeps up a brave face and as I leave she takes solace by ringing her young tennis coach and arranging some all night training sessions. |
| Apr 3rd | Plymouth. | | As we set sail from Blighty our spirits are high. The crew indulge in a little deck tennis. Three of them drown, as H.M.S. Conqueror is a submarine. |
| Apr 6th | Somewhere at sea. | | No sign of the Argies yet. I begin to suspect a trap, until the navigator points out that we have only just passed Ireland. |
| Apr 7th | Somewhere else at sea. | | Well, I'm afraid nothing much happened again today. We are managing an average of ten knots, though I still can't do one of those half-hitch double-reef jobs. I am increasingly convinced that the submarine is making a funny noise - a sort of 'Pip' ... 'Pip' ... 'Pip'. |
| Apr 10th | Still at bloody sea. | | Got up. Watched videos. Er... that's it. |
| Apr 12th | " | | God this is boring. |
| Apr 14th | " | | I mean, we've got 8,000 miles of this! |
| Apr 17-23rd | " | | I just can't stand it. Day after day. Nothing ever happens. |
| Apr 26th | " | | Attacked by a giant squid! There we were, innocently cruising along at a depth of 20,000 leagues, when suddenly everything turned into black and white and we were grasped by these huge tentacles, so we fired a harpoon at it but it just bounced off and then it attacked again and we all rocked back and forward and grabbed onto a handrail, and the next thing we knew the submarine had turned into a little plastic model that was obviously in an aquarium, but then the squid came back and one of its tentacles came crashing through a porthole, and water came gushing in an it looked as if we were all going to die until someone turned a great big valve thing and somehow everything was alright. |
| Apr 27th | " | | Wake up with a splitting headache. Discover our entire rum rations have been consumed. Please ignore that bit about the giant squid. |
| Apr 30th | " | | We have been at sea for over a month now. There is still no sign of the enemy, and I am becoming increasingly concerned for my crew. It cannot be easy for so many young, able-bodied men to be cooped up together with no prospect of any action - although some of the chaps seem to be coping admirably. Pettit and Cummings deserve particular mention, being quite happy to spend entire days confined to their quarters. I have frequently heard them moaning and groaning, and yet they have never once complained about seasickness. My only concern is their inexplicable sniggering every time I give the command 'Up periscope'. |
| May 1st | Land Ahoy! | | At last! We have finally arrived at our destination! I was beginning to despair of ever seeing land again, until I remember we were underwater. I immediately gave the order to surface and there, before us, rising from the ocean like two tiny insignificant bits of rock sticking out of the sea, lay the Falklands. We drop anchor and await orders from Downing Street. |
| May 2nd (9.00am) | Mal Vinas | | Mrs Thatcher issues an urgent message instructing us to abide strictly by the rules of conflict, in particular the 200 mile exclusion zone. She ties it to a carrier pigeon, and shoots it just in case. |
| May 2nd (9.01am) | " | | We receive another message by telephone. Mrs Thatcher informs us that the conflict is at a crisis point. A Peruvian Peace Plan has been sighted and is believed to be heading towards an acceptable agreement. It must be intercepted and destroyed at all costs. |
| May 2nd (2.00pm) | A long, long way from the exclusion zone. | | The Belgrano is now in our sights. However, it is heading away from the Task Force, so I suggest that we cannot attack unless it changes course. |
| May 2nd (2.01pm) | " | | We receive Mrs Thatcher's response. The Belgrado has changed course, and is now heading for the bottom of the sea. |

*\* On second thoughts, perhaps you'd better stick it in an envelope and put it somewhere where no one will ever see it - how about The Business Section of The Sunday Times.*

---

**MEMO**

TO: Foreign Secretary

FROM: The PM

DATE: April 22nd. 1982    TIME: 04.30

What's going on? Here I am trying to cut costs all over the place and I find out we're guarding some crappy little islands in the South Pacific! Get that Royal Navy Frigate out of there AT ONCE - we need something to check lobster pots round Lundi. As for those two wretched islands, give them back to the Argies ASAP, with a small cash incentive if necess...

---

*Ooh look what I found under my mattress.*

---

**Telephone Message**

TIME RECIEVED: 4.32    DATE: 2/4/82

FOR: PM    FROM: Mr Rex Hunt

OF: Governor/Falklands

RE: Unexpected Invasion

CALL BACK ☑    WILL CALL YOU ☐

TAKEN BY: [signature]

*This is Margaret Thatcher's first cabinet pictured soon after she swept to power in 1979. But what happened to the men behind the Iron Lady? We tracked them down and asked...*

# Where are they now?

## Cecil Parkinson
### aka Brett Python of the Chopperdales.

"After years of beavering away in my office, somebody walked in and caught us. On leaving the Government I took up a senior position in the Entertainment Industry and am currently available for Hen Nights, groups of pissed up WPCs and the Village People fan club although I'd rather not talk about that one."

## Kenneth Baker

"I was finally lured away from the world of politics when an unmissable opportunity arose to enter an allotment and nibble some lettuce leaves.

My career hit a difficult patch when I was briefly trapped in a ring of salt, but I've recently taken up an exciting new position half way up the wall of an outside toilet."

## Jeffrey Archer

"I am currently the world's greatest author, writing brilliant works of fiction such as this."

## Geoffrey Howe

"For me being a cabinet minister was merely a stepping stone on the career path towards my ultimate ambition – becoming a BR station announcer at Didcot Parkway. It's a fascinating job – for instance the 9.07 stopping service to Oxford was running approximately three minutes late the other day – it was one of those new ones where you push the sort of button thing to open the doors and it makes a whooshing sound, anyway it was my job to say it was late..."

## Roger Hunt

"After playing in the !966 World Cup Final, I had a brief spell as manager at Hartlepool before going on to open a sports shop. Nowadays I run my own pub and occasionally turn up in the wrong photo."

## Norman Tebbit

"After leaving the cabinet I suddenly realised how mistaken I'd been all along, and that basically people are like really nice, yeah? I mean if they're like just given a chance you know, so anyway I've taken up this voluntary position as Social Worker-in-residence at the Lambeth Community Resources Centre for Ethnic Minorities of Non Gender-specific Sexual Orientation."

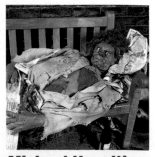

## Michael Heseltine

"As you can see, I'm still extremely successful, my career is going exactly according to plan and I certainly didn't blow it by standing for the leadership and ending up as a sad old loser with no political future... Any spare change guv?"

## John Major

We were unable to discover the present whereabouts of this anonymous little man.

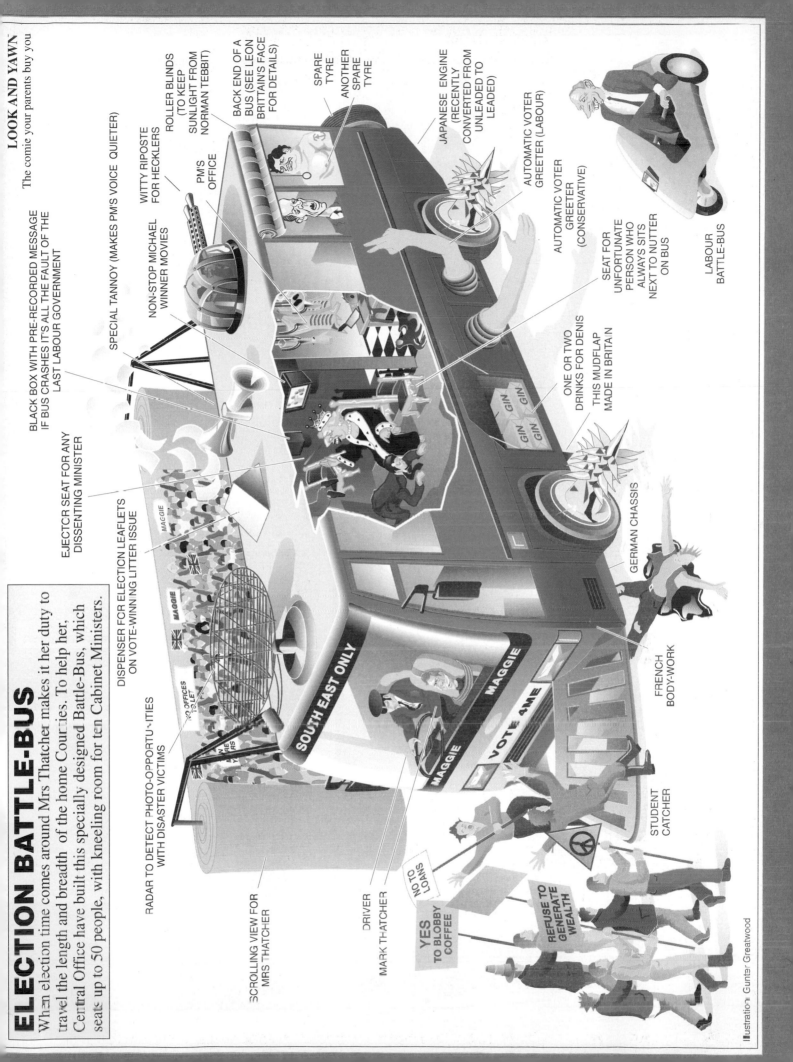

# ELECTION BATTLE-BUS

**LOOK AND YAWN**
The comic your parents buy you

When election time comes around Mrs Thatcher makes it her duty to travel the length and breadth of the home Counties. To help her, Central Office have built this specially designed Battle-Bus, which seats up to 50 people, with kneeling room for ten Cabinet Ministers.

BLACK BOX WITH PRE-RECORDED MESSAGE IF BUS CRASHES IT'S ALL THE FAULT OF THE LAST LABOUR GOVERNMENT

ROLLER BLINDS (TO KEEP SUNLIGHT FROM NORMAN TEBBIT)

WITTY RIPOSTE FOR HECKLERS

PM'S OFFICE

SPECIAL TANNOY (MAKES PM'S VOICE QUIETER)

NON-STOP MICHAEL WINNER MOVIES

EJECTOR SEAT FOR ANY DISSENTING MINISTER

DISPENSER FOR ELECTION LEAFLETS ON VOTE-WINNING LITTER ISSUE

SPARE TYRE

ANOTHER SPARE TYRE

JAPANESE ENGINE (RECENTLY CONVERTED FROM UNLEADED TO LEADED)

AUTOMATIC VOTER GREETER (LABOUR)

AUTOMATIC VOTER GREETER (CONSERVATIVE)

BACK END OF A BUS (SEE LEON BRITTAIN'S FACE FOR DETAILS)

SEAT FOR UNFORTUNATE PERSON WHO ALWAYS SITS NEXT TO NUTTER ON BUS

ONE OR TWO DRINKS FOR DENIS

THIS MUDFLAP MADE IN BRITAIN

GERMAN CHASSIS

GIN GIN GIN

LABOUR BATTLE-BUS

RADAR TO DETECT PHOTO-OPPORTUNITIES WITH DISASTER VICTIMS

SCROLLING VIEW FOR MRS THATCHER

DRIVER

MARK THATCHER

SOUTH EAST ONLY

MAGGIE

MAGGIE

MAGGIE

VOTE 4 ME

FRENCH BODY-WORK

STUDENT CATCHER

NO TO LOANS

YES TO BLOBBY COFFEE

REFUSE TO GENERATE WEALTH

Illustration Gunter Greatwood

Following the success of the English Civil War Society there is now a chance for you to spend your weekends re-creating some more of Britain's historic battles. Join...

# The miners' strike re-enactment society

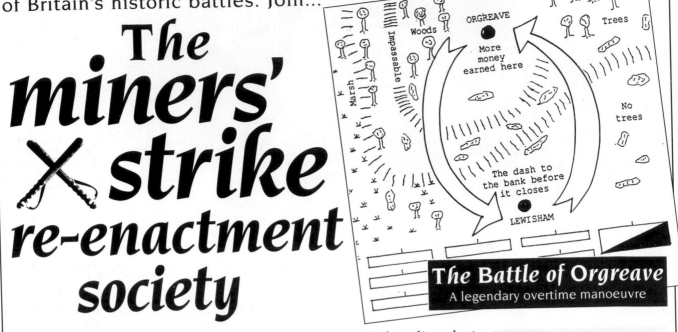

ORGREAVE

Woods

Trees

Marsh

Impassable

More money earned here

No trees

The dash to the bank before it closes

LEWISHAM

**The Battle of Orgreave**
A legendary overtime manoeuvre

Experience the roar of the strike-buster's lorry tearing out of the coking plant, the gallop of the mounted policemen, the drone of Arthur Scargill on a megaphone, as you run around a field re-creating history and looking stupid.

**Here are just a few of the parts you can play:**

### A Policeman

The policeman was the traditional foot soldier of the battles of 1984. With only seventy three policemen to every miner theirs was no easy task. They were also handicapped by having to carry around thousands of pounds of overtime money in their wallets.

### The flying picket

Your role in the re-enactment is to out-manoeuvre the combined police forces of England and Wales by standing in front of them as they charge at you on police horses... (Protective Gear of T-shirt and jeans provided)

### A Sun journalist

The journalist or 'hack' was a crucial ally of the Government forces and reported on every detail and horror of the battle as he saw it from his vantage point of the pub five miles away.

### Billy Bragg

Your job will be to go to Red Wedge concerts and say 'Like it's really bad, like, because, well, it's like not fair on the mining communities and like, all working people and stuff.'

### Member of Union of Democratic Mineworkers

As a member of the Union of Democratic miners, your job is to carry on working and help the government win the strike. Then be given the sack.

Part of your exciting weekend away will be spent visiting the spots where these great battles occurred – soak up the atmosphere of these ghostly deserted places known as 'South Wales' and 'The North'.

### How to get to the Miners' Strike Re-Enactment Weekend...

Take the M1 as far as Junction 7. Here you will be stopped by a police roadblock and sent home again.

### Total cost

In order that this is a true re-creation of this historic struggle we are offering this weekend at a realistic £4.5 billion. Payment can be made by cheque or credit card, or by us sequestrating every penny in your bank account.

Here are just some of the ordinary people who have already signed up to join the Miners' Strike Re-enactment Society

### Mr A Scargill from Barnsley

– seen here addressing a hall packed full of enthusiastic chairs – has a fairly mundane and unimportant job as President of the National Union of No-Miners. However, on weekends Arthur dresses up as the powerful leader Arthur Scargill. "I think I've managed to get the ridiculous hair style and silly high-pitched voice just right".

**P C Dimbleby** "I thought it would be interesting to play the part of a lesbian support group... You what? You lefty troublemakers you, take that... Ow, help my woman-space is being invaded by a truncheon-phallus... I'll give you truncheon phallus you pinko subversive you..."

# ONE BAD APPLE

Watch for P.C. 2345 — seen here at Orgreave behaving in a fair and proper manner.

## Paper sales up again!

Top hats off to our paper sellers at the following branches: W.H.Smtihs, Woking, where a record 17 copies of The Telegraph were sold! John Menzies, Chichester, with six copies and a regular standing order placed by Colonel Peregrine Arbuthnot (D.S.O. Retd). Sid's Kiosk, Jarrow, with a best ever total of one copy picked up by mistake, then put back again.

## It's run over a beggar week!

So — the pinko-liberal newspaper owners want us to clean up the City. Well let's start with the scum on the pavements!

**How YOU can help:**
- Get pissed on expensive champagne and run over a beggar on you way home.
- Set fire to his cardboard box!
- Fill his begging bowl with worthless currency e.g. Lire
- Make him a Lloyds Name.

## It's another Royal parasite!

So — yet another Royal baby has been born with a silver spoon in its greedy mouth, looking forward to an over-priviledged life of private nannies, expensive education and skiing holidays, all at the expense of the ordinary tax payer. Well good for him!

## STOP THE NHS!

Assemble 10 a.m. Cabinet Room. Close down the hospitals and bring the N.H.S. to a standstill!

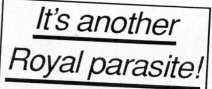

## UPPER CLASS WAR

BRITAINS MOST UNRULY TABLOID

PRICE ON APPLICATION

No. 10

# HOW TO SPLIT THE NUM!

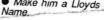

INSIDE: SACK AN EMPLOYEE AND WIN A PORSCHE!

*private grief*

...ws at Ten Weather

## SHYTE ONE

9.00 World Wrestling Foundation Mega-wrestle mania. 10.00 Isn't this the channel that has The Simpsons? 10.30 Truck-asaurus. Featuring head to head truck'n'tractor crushin'. 11.00 It must be The Simpsons soon. 11.30 Luv at first bonk. Sexy guys'n'gals in blind date grope-athon! 1.00 No sign of The Simpsons, yet. 2.00 Mateys Australian soap about life in a cheap set. 3.00 Still not The Simpsons, which was the only reason you got that bloody dish. 4.00 Lose your limbs! High risk game show. 6.00 The Simpsons – at last! (The one you saw on that tape you borrowed.)

## THE MOVIE CHANNEL

6am CASABLANCA (1973) Questionable remake of the Bogart classic. Stars Bernard Cribbins and Hannah Gordon.
8am TEEN RAVE USA (1978) True to life teen-pic. A group of Californian teenagers want to drive around with pretty girls and listen to rock'n'roll. But being teenagers they're too spotty and self conscious to do anything about it.
9.45am DRACULA – THE TRUE STORY (1971) 1970s Hammer Horror. Genuinely terrifying flares and sideburns.
12noon DAD'S ARMY RIDES AGAIN (1989) Second film of the succesful TV sit-com does as well as can be expected with the remaining cast. Good opening scene of Private Pike looking out of the window and seeing the rest of the platoon killed by a doodlebug.
3pm THE PLAGIARISER (1990) An actor who looks a bit like Arnold Schwarzennegger in a plot that looks a bit like The Terminator except very cheap and badly made.
5.45pm ENTERTAINMENT TONITE Previews of tonight's Shyte movies – giving away the entire plot of every one.
7.55pm ENTERTAINMENT TOMORROW Previews of tomorrow's Entertainment Tonite, previewing the previews of tomorrow's movies.
11.30pm NOT MUCH ENTERTAINMENT ALL WEEK, ACTUALLY Preview of all the week's forthcoming movie previews, look there's a lot of time to fill alright, I mean they've only made so many films...
2.45am ERASERHEAD (1979) Very slow black and white film we always put on really late so you fall asleep and spill your lager down your shirt.

## SHYTE MOVIES PLUS

12.00am – 12.00pm. All the decent films but all fuzzy and scrambled because you can't afford the decoder anymore.

## CHILDREN'S CHANNEL

8.00 Cartoon fun. 9.00 Non-stop cartoon capers. 11.30 Children develop bags under their eyes. 12.30 They become very irritable. 2.30 They hit the cat with the lego mallet. 3.30 You suggest playing out in the garden. 3.31 They hit *you* with the lego mallet. 3.32 You fall to the floor stunned. 3.33 Kids switch to German porn channel.

## ADULT CHANNEL

12.00 Check wife is asleep. 12.05 Fetch decoder from hiding place under the carpet. 12.10 Watch a few sad German girls take their bras off. 12.15 Fetch box of tissues. 12.20 Join sleeping wife in bed.

# Dear CELIA

**CELIA PRIM** - THE AGONY AUNT WITH A REASSURINGLY SENSIBLE NAME

# Our sex-life is at a standstill

**Q** **DEAR CELIA: We have been married for 35 years and our sex life is virtually non-existent.** In fact, we have only ever had sex once, and on that occasion we were unlucky enough to produce twins. Lately I have started to enjoy the odd drink, and now I find I can no longer maintain an erection.

■ **DEAR ANXIOUS:** This is a very common problem, although it doesn't usually affect women.

**Q** Dear Celia: I am a forty year old man and, for the past twenty years, I have been living with my male lover. We share many mutual interests, such as wearing leather trousers, listening to Bronski Beat, growing droopy moustaches and going to 'Heaven' at weekends. We've always enjoyed a satisfying sexual relationship. Do you think I may be gay?
■ **DEAR SIMON:** It's probably just a phase you're going through.

## My teacher had sex with me

**Q** Dear Celia: I'm at my wits end. I'm fourteen years old and my teacher has got me pregnant. I've tried to talk to him about it but he refuses to have anything to do with me. I can't tell my family, because they're Catholics and would kill me if they knew what had happened. Anyway, my problem is -

## PHONE OUR AGONY LINES

| | |
|---|---|
| What is an orgasm? | 0898 316401 |
| Is it really? | 0898 316402 |
| How to find the clitoris | 0898 316403 |
| How to find the Penis | 0898 316404 |
| How to annoy Mrs M. Giles of 3, The Mews, Ascot | 0344 75142 |
| I think my memory's going | 0898 316405 |
| I think I have number blindness | 0898316316406 |
| I think my memory's going | 0898 316407 |
| I can't pay my phone bill | 0898 316408 |
| I think my house is on fire | 999 |

how do you get coffee stains out of curtains?
■ **CELIA SAYS:** Try a little bicarbonate of soda to which a drop of milk has been added. Don't forget to try it out on an inconspicuous area first!

**Q** Dear Celia: My parents have split up and I've just found out that I'm pregnant by my sister's boyfriend who beats her up but I can't tell him it's his baby because he knows about that money I took to get my brother out of trouble when he was on drugs. What can I do?
■ **CELIA SAYS:** Leave 'Brookside'.

**Q** Dear Celia: My problem is my husband. He is always interfering... No I'm not... Yes he is...

Don't listen to her... Let go... He's always undermining my confidence... Well it's not surprising if she writes crap letters like this... See he doesn't let me do anything... Give me that pen...
■ **CELIA SAYS:** Your husband sounds as if he needs help... I do not... Yes you do... That's a crap answer...

## My big boob nightmare

**Q** Dear Celia: I have a genuine emotional problem that doesn't involve sex at all, but you keep making up smutty headlines to trick people into reading it.
■ **DEAR BIG BOOBS:** Tough.

## HE CAN'T STOP IT

☆ I am a compulsive gambler and I keep losing money. P.S. I bet you a tenner you won't print this.

☆ I have inherited a small amount of money from a relative and have been told that a high rate preferential investment portfolio would be my best option. Am I on the right page?
■ **NO.**

❀❀❀❀❀❀❀❀❀❀

### Bouquet of the week

Dear Celia: I'd like to nominate Mrs E. Foster of 32, Lansdowne Close, Gloucester for this week's bouquet, as I run a nearby flower shop and it would save me having to deliver the one her husband ordered.

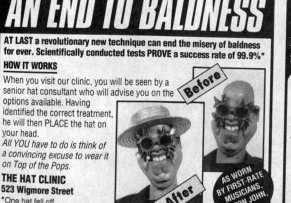

## Bank of England PLC
### THREADBARE St LONDON EC2

The Government
~~10-11 Downing Street~~
~~London W1~~

*go. the Bundesbank Germany*

Statement
1979-1993
Sheet
471

Is this the correct address for your financial details to be sent?
If not, please amend.

Description of entries
(C) Credit   (D) Debit

| Description | Amount |
|---|---|
| British Aerospace payment recd. Thank you | £390million (C) |
| Tax cuts for posh people | £billions (D) |
| British Steel sale payment recd. Thank you | £2.4 billion (C) |
| Yet more tax cuts | £even more billions (D) |
| Even more tax cuts | £whatever was left (D) |
| B.P. sale payment recd. Thank you | £6.1 billion (C) |
| Foreign aid standing order********Cancelled as per instruction******** | |
| British Gas sale payment recd. Thank you | £5.2 billion (C) |
| Rover (sweetner a/c) | £44.4 million (D) |
| Water authority sale payment recd. Thank you | £3.5 billion (C) |
| M.I.5 | £???? (D) |
| British Telecom sale payment recd. Thank you | £390 million (C) |
| Social security (Scrounging bastards a/c) | £800 billion (D) |
| Health service account | £29 billion (D) |
| National Girobank sale payment recd. Thank you | £112 million (C) |
| Introduction and immediate abolition of poll-tax | £1 billion (D) |
| North Sea oil & gas revenue payment recd. Thank you | £71 billion (C) |
| Electricity Board sale payment recd. Thank you | £5.2 billion (C) |
| Some Greek speculator on black wednesday | £1 billion (D) |
| Electricity Generating Co. sale payment recd. Thank you | £2.2 billion (C) |
| Blackpool prom autobank 11pm | £50 (D) |
| Standard Tandoori, Blackpool | £48.20 (D) |
| | |
| **Balance carried forward** | £50billion (D) |

## why I'm such a success in Britain

A note of encouragement to the UK's top management

各種学会社は ション の 予定 が 保健機関〈WHO 横浜 で 開催 する イス 会議」に は 世界 から 訪れ る 食施設 でも ウイ 感染者 もいる は ト 免疫不全ウイ の コンベンション 技設 が 問 われる

## BUSIN

Business Editor: Ron Citistaff

# FURTHER LOSSES FO LLOYD'S NAMES

The Government were under rene
pressure today to bail out the Llo
Names after revelations that they
lost a further seven million on a tri
Ascot racecourse.

Shocked investors watched in disbelie
their chosen horses failed to come in f
every time and give them a ten thousand
cent return on their investments.

"I can't even begin to count my losses," sob
one investor. "Because I'm far too stupid;
I'm sure it's pots of cash." Another add
"Last year I came here and made a fortune
picking the right horse. But this year n
selection came in last and no-one will give n
my money back. It's just not fair."

Now Mary Archer has set up anoth
hardship fund to try and help the victims
the 'Lloyds Names Wrong Horse Affair'.
was thinking about doing some charity wor
for Oxfam or the Homeless or something bu
helping a load of greedy snobs who for onc
lost a few bob is a much more deservin
cause" said the tragically misguided novelist's
wife.

## Bank of England P.
### THREADBARE St LONDON EC2

The Government
10-11 Downing Street
London SW1

Dear Mr Government,

We see from our records that your indebtedness
to this bank is £49,999,999,750 over your
agreed overdraft limit of £250. I am therefore
requesting that you stop using your account
forthwith and return your cheque card and
chequebook.

You have been charged £20 for this letter

Yours sincerely

Mr Theobald, Assistant Manager

## Today on the stock exchange

Today lots of people
spent most of the time
shouting and pointing
and being really
aggressive. Most of them
made funny gestures to
overweight people who
shouted into two
telephones at once. I
couldn't get what they
were saying but generally
it sort of sounded like
'Cragghhhh rubarb
rubarb, sell, no buy, I
think I'm having a heart
attack". Then they all
had too much to drink at
lunchtime and were very
rude to some poor
people before going on to
several clubs and having
an affair.

### Our Motto

## "One Law for the Rich"

### A message from your Governor...

"May I welcome you to *Ford Open Prison*.

I hope that during your stay here you will take advantage of our excellent facilities such as the casino and cocktail lounge, and enjoy the gourmet cuisine which has helped us win the much coveted Michelin 'Prison of the Year' Award."

### The Regime

*Ford Open Prison* believes in rehabilitation through discipline, hard work and fine brandies.

The prison routine must be strictly adhered to at all times:

**7:00** Early morning call. All cells to be slopped out and spotlessly clean by

**7:15.** (If the warders are disturbing you whilst doing this please inform Reception.)

**7:30** Buffet breakfast in the Maxwell Suite.

**8:00** Exercise period (Golf clubs available for hire.)

**11:25** Work Duty.

**11:30** Luncheon.

**3:55** A bit more work.

**4:00** Tea (on the lawn when fine).

**5:00** Counselling Session in the Clubroom; any prisoner will be able to talk frankly about his problems to a professional judge or politician.

**7:30** Dinner in the Great Hall (black tie).

**8:00** You are released and taken by limo straight to your safe deposit box in Knightsbridge.

### What they say...

*Wonderful medical facilities, cured me of my Altzheimer's disease – E Saunders*

*Excellent training facilities, I picked up a ludicrously well-paid job within hours of my release – G Ronson*

### Punitive measures

Never forget you're here to pay your debt to society, and therefore expect to suffer some loss of liberty.

The following restrictions will apply:

1 Butlers may not be used to reserve loungers around the swimming pool

2 Champagne buckets must be slopped out every day

3 No more than two mistresses per night

4 Due to overcrowding, it is now three to a cellphone

5 Private helicopters must land and take off within reasonable hours

Failure to obey these rules may lead to the loss of certain privileges such as: the well-stocked mini-bar in your cell, Red Hot Dutch ...ers, Snout

Lord Longford

Although *Ford* is an 'open' prison, there is still considerable security and I'm pleased to say we have never had any riff-raff break into the establishment.

### Old Fordonians

Sadly, your stay in *Ford Open Prison* is likely to be all too short: but why not maintain your links with the old place, and help other rising young fraudsters, by becoming an Old Fordonian.

For just £50,000, or an hour's wages,

**Stop Press**
We strongly recommend that no subscription money be sent to 'The Old Fordonians' as this whole organisation is just a scam by one of our prisoners and is being investigated by the Serious Fraud Office.

(Havana thigh-rolled cigars) and being exempt from visits by

whichever's more, we will send you this lovely tie and a subscription to our newsletter 'The Ex-Con'.

---

★★★

FRIDAY MAY 2.754th   **33**

# ...SS DAY

## THE BIT YOU LEAVE ON THE TRAIN SEAT

# Millions unlikely to read this page

...SINESS EDITOR Ron Citistaff was shocked by the revelation ...t nobody found this city section the least bit interesting and ...ders were highly likely to pull this page out and leave it on the ...in seat.

...t's not dull. It isn't dull. Not dull at all. I certainly don't find it ...and neither does my wife... hey why are you walking away?" ...ell let's face it if you're still reading this you're probably on a ...ish Rail train somewhere pretending you understand what the ...g Seng Index is for. I bet you're shouting into a cellphone all ...way to East Croydon. Look why not just admit it – you were ... three months ago but still tell the wife you're going to work.

## Man in City wears collar that matches his shirt

Shares plunged in the city today when a stockbroker was discovered in a collar that matched the rest of his shirt. Detectives on the scene believe there must have been a mix up with somebody else's shirt during the rush hour. An appeal has been issued for the owner of the other shirt to come forward and swap collars.

"100% NOT VERY FUNNY"  KAK

## CITY NEWS IN BRIEF

We're all fucked

### STOP PRESS

## No more interesting stories

Readers of this paper were disappointed just now when they turned the paper on it's side in a last ditch attempt to find something interesting on this page.

# CANARY WHARF

## *A development that stands alone*

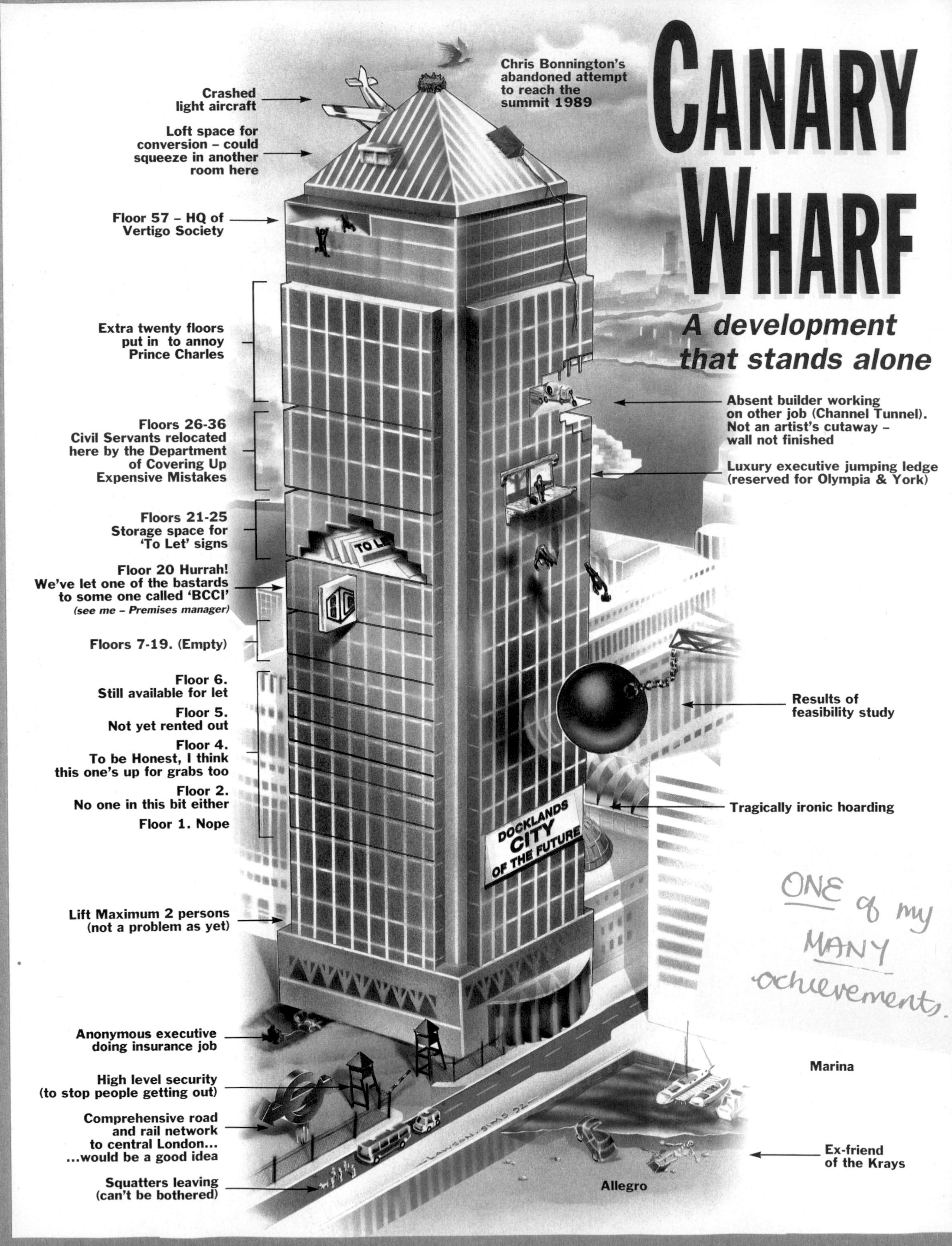

**Chris Bonnington's abandoned attempt to reach the summit 1989**

**Crashed light aircraft**

**Loft space for conversion – could squeeze in another room here**

**Floor 57 – HQ of Vertigo Society**

**Extra twenty floors put in to annoy Prince Charles**

**Floors 26-36 Civil Servants relocated here by the Department of Covering Up Expensive Mistakes**

**Floors 21-25 Storage space for 'To Let' signs**

**Floor 20 Hurrah! We've let one of the bastards to some one called 'BCCI'** *(see me – Premises manager)*

**Floors 7-19. (Empty)**

**Floor 6. Still available for let**

**Floor 5. Not yet rented out**

**Floor 4. To be Honest, I think this one's up for grabs too**

**Floor 2. No one in this bit either**

**Floor 1. Nope**

**Lift Maximum 2 persons (not a problem as yet)**

**Anonymous executive doing insurance job**

**High level security (to stop people getting out)**

**Comprehensive road and rail network to central London… …would be a good idea**

**Squatters leaving (can't be bothered)**

**Absent builder working on other job (Channel Tunnel). Not an artist's cutaway – wall not finished**

**Luxury executive jumping ledge (reserved for Olympia & York)**

**Results of feasibility study**

**Tragically ironic hoarding**

**Marina**

**Ex-friend of the Krays**

*ONE of my MANY achievements.*

**TO LET**

**DOCKLANDS CITY OF THE FUTURE**

**Allegro**

# Application for state handout (Revised)

Form SCRO/UNG(e)/R

You must fill in this form correctly if you want to claim unemployment benefit. Please write in BLOCK CAPITALS. in ancient Taoist script. If English is not your first language, then you are probably the Duke of Edinburgh and already get loads of tax payers money. This form will be kept **strictly** private and confidential, although we can't answer for the hundreds of photocopies that will be circulated round the police, Inland Revenue, neighbours etc.

## 1. ABOUT YOU

**YOUR NAME:**

Surname

Other names

see note 1

**YOUR ADDRESS:**

Postcode

see note 2

**YOUR PREVIOUS OCCUPATION:**

- ☐ Skilled worker
- ☐ Ex-Skilled worker forced to deliver pizza leaflets
- ☐ Ex-Skilled worker turned self-employed cider tester in park

**HOME PHONE NO:**

see note 3

**WORK PHONE NO:**

see note 4

**DO YOU HAVE ANY RELATIVES?**
No ☐     Yes ☐
see note 5

**ARE YOU REGISTERED DISABLED?**
No ☐     Yes ☐
see note 6     see note 7

**HAVE YOU A PARTNER LIVING WITH YOU?**
No ☐     Yes ☐
see note 8     see note 9

**DO YOU HAVE ANY SAVINGS?**
No ☐     Yes ☐
see note 10     see note 11

**ARE YOU LYING TO US?**
No ☐     Yes ☐
see note 12     see note 13

**YOU DON'T KNOW THE MEANING OF THE WORDS 'HARD WORK' DO YOU?**
No ☐

**WOULD YOU BE PREPARED TO TAKE ANY WORK OFFERED TO YOU, NO MATTER HOW POORLY PAID, DEGRADING & MENIAL**
No ☐     Yes ☐
see note 14     see note 15

**DO YOU LIKE TICKING BOXES?**
Yes ☐ ☐ ☐ ☐ ☐ ☐ ☐
No ☐

**ARE YOU LIKELY TO TURN UP AT THE BENEFIT OFFICE WITH A CAN OF SPECIAL BREW, SCREAMING THAT YOU CAN'T GO ON LIVING LIKE THIS, AND THROWING A CHAIR AT THE GLASS SCREEN?**
No ☐     Yes ☐
see note 16

## 2. YOUR BENEFIT (See note 17)

ASSUMING YOU'VE GOT THIS FAR, DO YOU WISH TO CLAIM:

a) The hard-earned money which you clearly don't deserve

b) A strong sense of moral superiority afforded by nobly declining state hand-outs on principle
see note 18

TICK HERE IF YOU ALSO WISH TO CLAIM FREE NHS SPECTACLES ☐
see note 19

WOULD YOU LIKE HELP WITH HEATING?
Yes ☐
see note 20

## DECLARATION

(Remember, to give false information is a very serious offence – unless of course you are Minister of Employment, in which case it's essential)

I admit to not being capable of standing on my own two feet, and hereby claim a sad life of never-ending dependency with no prospect for self-improvement. I am a worm.

LAST CHANCE TO CHANGE YOUR MIND

BUGGER. GO ON THEN, SIGN HERE (FULL NAME)

## OUR PROMISE

We promise to process this claim within 28 days. Though exactly which 28 days is up to us.

## NOTES

**1** Come on, your real name. We know what you're up to.

**2** Ha! Now we know where you live, we can keep an eye on you. You might have to keep up that fake limp for a long time.

**3** Not so poor that you can't afford a phone, eh?

**4** Gotcha? That's your claim for unemployment done for.

**5** Well why can't they look after you? Must you always come running to us? Claim disallowed.

**6** You soon will be if you don't find yourself a job, you lazy bastard.

**7** Claim disallowed – and don't bother coming in to complain, we've got steps up to the office heh heh.

**8** I'm not surprised! Who'd find a loser like you attractive?

**9** Claim disallowed

**10** You obviously can't be trusted with money. Claim disallowed

**11** Well spend your own bloody money first. Claim disallowed

**12** Oh yes you are. Claim disallowed

**13** Claim disallowed

**14** Claim disallowed

**15** God, you've really got no self-respect left, have you, you scrounging little bastard. I pity you

**16** Claim disallowed. You are a member of staff

**17** Not yet, it's not

**18** Jolly good! That certainly saves on paperwork

**19** Aha! Got you! You obviously don't need them if you can read that tiny print. Claim disallowed

**20** Then burn this form

## OFFICIAL USE ONLY

Claim disallowed ☐

Claim not allowed ☐

Claim unallowed ☐

Claim rejected ☐

Claim turned down ☐     Claim lost ☐

## CHANGE TO STATISTICS

Please note we have made a number of minor changes to the way we define "unemployment". Scroungers–er–clients no longer count as unemployed if they are:

**1** Over 60 (months old)

**2** Humanoid

**3** Someone without a job

Unemployment – scourge of a nation. Nothing saps the dignity of a man like having nothing to do (Doris told me this). This is how I reduced the Dole Queues.

# Club 18-90

## It's a party by the seaside

## EVENING ENTERTAINMENT

After a hectic day you can enjoy our rib-tickling revue show entitled 'The Labour Party are a lot of silly chumps' featuring a rewritten version of Hello Dolly which we've wittily called 'The Conservative Party are the best party for the future of Britain and you should definitely vote for us and not Labour. Dolly.'

## FACILITIES FOR BABIES

If your secretary suddenly goes into labour there are ample facilities for rushing her out of the town buying her silence with a combination of cash offers and threats from Special Branch.
**If you would like a week at Club 18-90 just ring for a brochure by dialling 0800 and asking for Freephone Nuremberg.**

### Yes!

Whatever your appallingly-right-wing views, get away from the real world for a week with our amazing Club 18-90 Conference Holiday Offer.

Take your pick from our huge choice of just the one resort and enjoy the sort of piss-up you haven't had since well – the last conference. This year we're laying on even more exciting activities than ever including:
Standing ovations, Clapping, Applauding, Enthusiastically putting your hands together,
Slapping your palms energetically,
Waving the Union Jack

**Imagine a typical day at Club 18-90.** You are woken by room service knocking at your door so you quickly usher your secretary down the fire escape out the back. After a leisurely read through the Daily Telegraph to see if you were photographed hovering behind an important minister you can stroll down to the specially built atmospherically controlled Conference Centre. Once inside the Centre you are completely protected from the outside world in every way. There are no poor people, or people who might disagree with you or shatter your narrow and bigoted view of the world.

Then why not take a wander round our conveniently situated souvenir stall? The variety of gifts is endless. There are Maggie plates, Maggie mugs, Maggie clocks, I ♥ Maggie car stickers, large air balloons in the shape of Maggie and a Ted Heath Pencil case. Too much luncheon will be served in The Fulklands Banqueting Suite and comes with obsequious waiters who apologise when you complain that the gazpacho's cold. Any vegetarians should let us know beforehand so that they can be refused entry.

Our famous Bluecoats are specially trained to make sure the day goes without a hitch, and will keep you amused for hours on end with their hilarious 'The recovery is on the way' routine and cheeky catchphrase 'We fully support the Prime Minister'.

There are no end of clubs and societies you can join during your week to keep you amused – The No Turning Back Group, the Right Way Forward Group, the No-Way Right Back to Forwards Group, the Eugene Terreblanche Vigilante Lebensraum Contra Freedom Armband-that-looks-a-bit-like-a-swastika Front, and The National Trust.

## KIDS

And don't worry about the kids! They can join our super children's club the Young Conservatives. We organise Food-Throwing competitions at local Indian restaurants and other fun and games like the 'Wubbly-chin Contest, Kicking the Tramp, and 'Puke In the Cab!'

### Accommodation

**Your choice of hotels...**

### The Imperial Grand Posh Snobby Hotel

Part of the International 'Snobby' Hotel Group, suitable for Cabinet ministers, heads of industry, newspaper editors and anyone who basically isn't having to pay for this out of their own pocket. Large luxury rooms with en-suite bathroom features WC, bath, shower, double washbasin and bidet for well, your feet obviously, I mean you might easily have grubby feet, say if you've been doing a lot of walking without shoes on, oh dear I've gone all red.

### The Large Bland New Hotel

Part of the Novotel Trust House Granada Group of Exactly the Same Hotels. This is conveniently located on a huge roundabout about five miles out of town, within walking distance of the 24-hour garage. Ideal for delegates in sales, computers, and Mr By-rite suit. Full irritating menu that says things like Steakburger 'n' Bar-b-Beans, and Fisherman's platter 'n' fries 'n' dip. Features muzak in the bar, the foyer, in the lifts aaaarggghhh I just can't stand this bland soulless noise anymore...

### The Sea View

**Patron – A. Bigot**
Slightly more basic accommodation for the ordinary delegate. Rooms have hot and cold running water (down the walls), tasteful 1960s wardrobes and non matching bedside table and statutory grubby chair. Beds include carefully concealed metal corner of frame under bedspread guaranteed to gash your shins first thing in morning.
Choice of breakfast cereals, but no choice of which dreadful couple you get put with.
We regret no visitors after 1959.

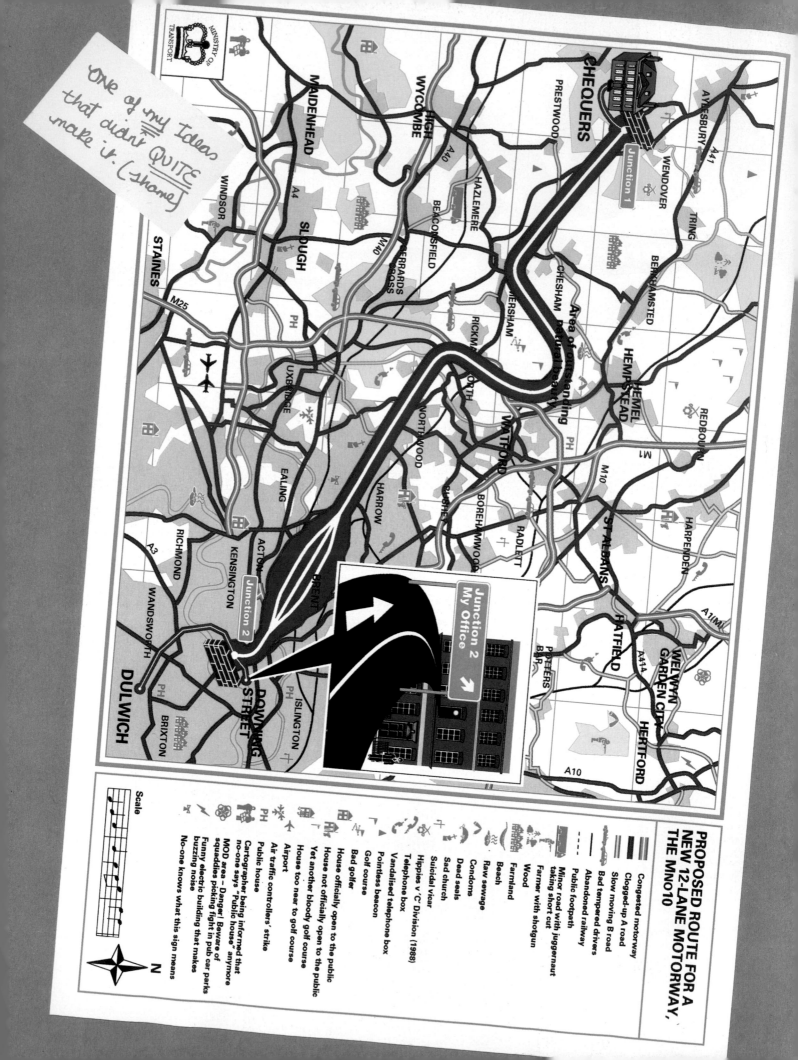

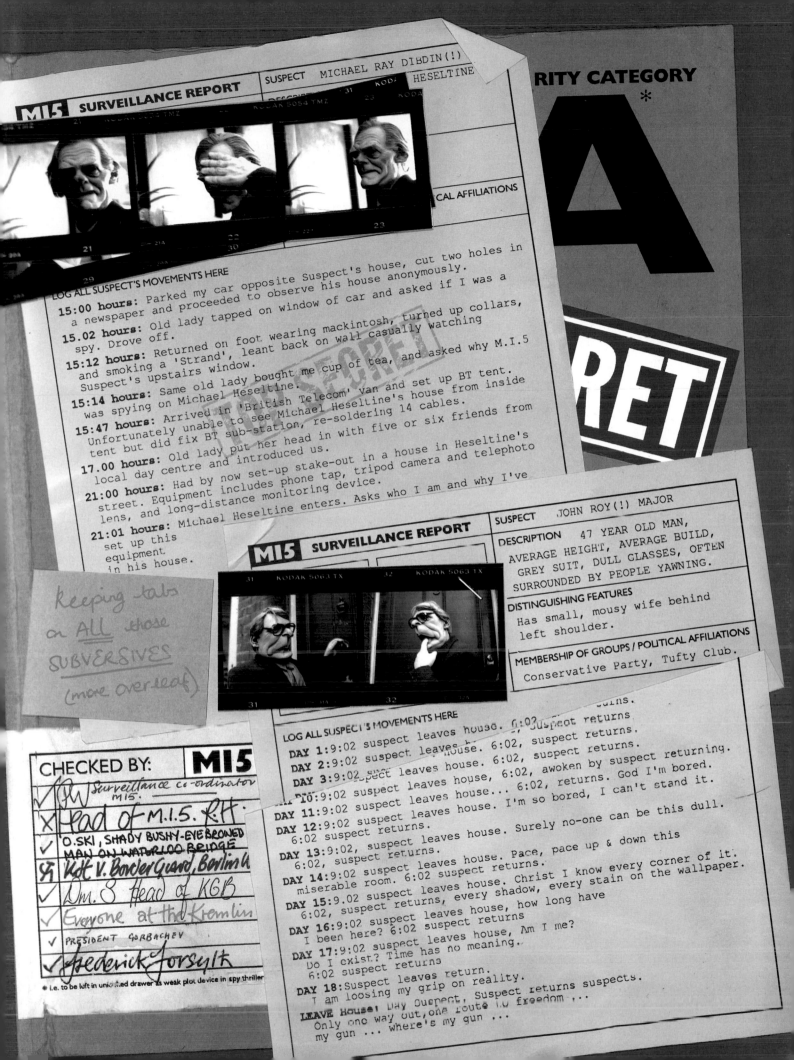

**MI5 SURVEILLANCE REPORT**

SUSPECT MICHAEL RAY DIBDIN(!) HESELTINE

DESCRIPTION ... 31 ...

... CAL AFFILIATIONS

**RITY CATEGORY**
*
**A**
**RET**

**STRICTLY TOP SECRET**

**LOG ALL SUSPECT'S MOVEMENTS HERE**

**15:00 hours:** Parked my car opposite Suspect's house, cut two holes in a newspaper and proceeded to observe his house anonymously.

**15.02 hours:** Old lady tapped on window of car and asked if I was a spy. Drove off.

**15.12 hours:** Returned on foot wearing mackintosh, turned up collars, and smoking a 'Strand', leant back on wall casually watching Suspect's upstairs window.

**15:14 hours:** Same old lady bought me cup of tea, and asked why M.I.5 was spying on Michael Heseltine.

**15:47 hours:** Arrived in 'British Telecom' van and set up BT tent. Unfortunately unable to see Michael Heseltine's house from inside tent but did fix BT sub-station, re-soldering 14 cables.

**17.00 hours:** Old lady put her head in with five or six friends from local day centre and introduced us.

**21:00 hours:** Had by now set-up stake-out in a house in Heseltine's street. Equipment includes phone tap, tripod camera and telephoto lens, and long-distance monitoring device.

**21:01 hours:** Michael Heseltine enters. Asks who I am and why I've set up this equipment in his house.

*Keeping tabs on ALL those SUBVERSIVES (more overleaf)*

**MI5 SURVEILLANCE REPORT**

SUSPECT JOHN ROY(!) MAJOR

DESCRIPTION 47 YEAR OLD MAN, AVERAGE HEIGHT, AVERAGE BUILD, GREY SUIT, DULL GLASSES, OFTEN SURROUNDED BY PEOPLE YAWNING.

DISTINGUISHING FEATURES
Has small, mousy wife behind left shoulder.

MEMBERSHIP OF GROUPS / POLITICAL AFFILIATIONS
Conservative Party, Tufty Club.

**LOG ALL SUSPECT'S MOVEMENTS HERE**

**DAY 1:** 9:02 suspect leaves house. 6:02, suspect returns.

**DAY 2:** 9:02 suspect leaves house. 6:02, suspect returns.

**DAY 3:** 9:02 suspect leaves house, 6:02, awoken by suspect returning.

**DAY 10:** 9:02 suspect leaves house... 6:02, returns. God I'm bored.

**DAY 11:** 9:02 suspect leaves house. I'm so bored, I can't stand it.

**DAY 12:** 9:02 suspect leaves house. Surely no-one can be this dull. 6:02 suspect returns.

**DAY 13:** 9:02, suspect leaves house. Pace, pace up & down this miserable room. 6:02 suspect returns.

**DAY 14:** 9:02 suspect leaves house. Christ I know every corner of it, every shadow, every stain on the wallpaper.

**DAY 15:** 9.02 suspect leaves house, how long have 6:02, suspect returns.

**DAY 16:** 9:02 suspect leaves house, how long have I been here? 6:02 suspect returns

**DAY 17:** 9:02 suspect leaves house, Am I me? Do I exist? Time has no meaning. 6:02 suspect returns

**DAY 18:** Suspect leaves return. I am loosing my grip on reality.

**LEAVE House!** Day Suspect, Suspect returns suspects. Only one way out, one route t.o freedom ... my gun ... where's my gun ...

**CHECKED BY:** **MI5**

✓ Surveillance co-ordinator MI5.
✗ Head of M.I.5. R.H.
✓ O.SKI, SHADY BUSHY-EYEBROWED MAN ON WATERLOO BRIDGE
✓ Kgt V. Border Guard, Berlin W.
✓ Dm. 8 Head of KGB
✓ Everyone at the Kremlin
✓ PRESIDENT GORBACHEV
✓ Frederick Forsyth

* i.e. to be left in unlocked drawer as weak plot device in spy thriller

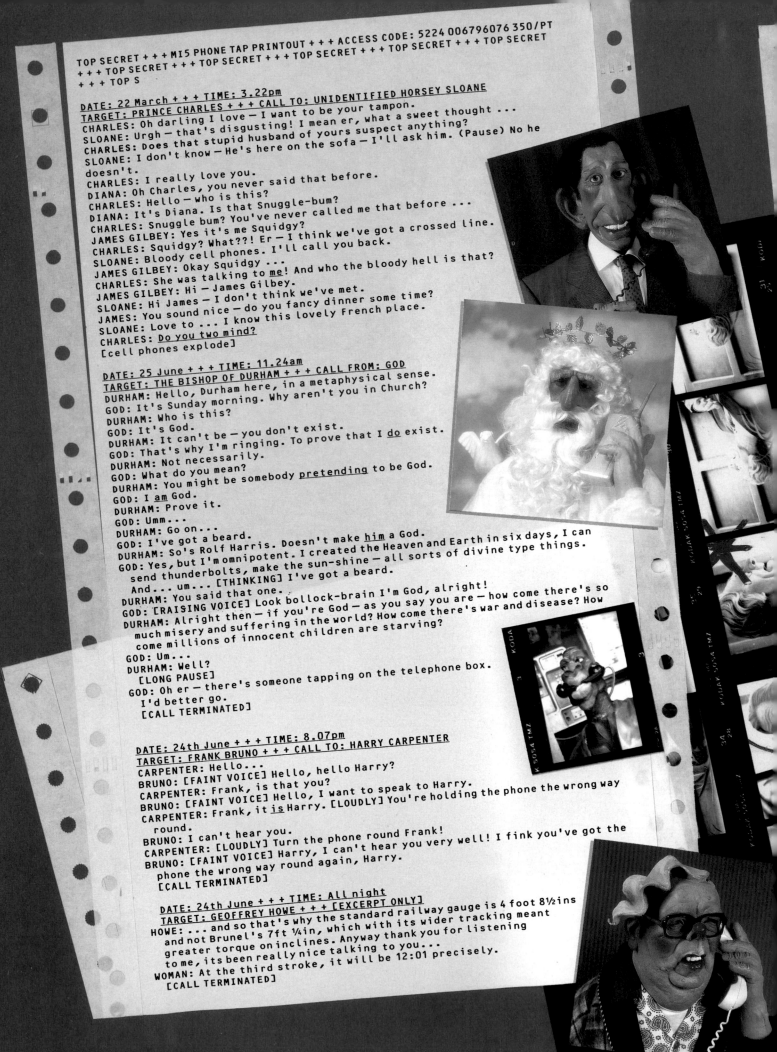

DATE: 22 March + + + TIME: 3.22pm
TARGET: PRINCE CHARLES + + + CALL TO: UNIDENTIFIED HORSEY SLOANE
CHARLES: Oh darling I love — I want to be your tampon.
SLOANE: Urgh — that's disgusting! I mean er, what a sweet thought ...
CHARLES: Does that stupid husband of yours suspect anything?
SLOANE: I don't know — He's here on the sofa — I'll ask him. (Pause) No he
doesn't.
CHARLES: I really love you.
DIANA: Oh Charles, you never said that before.
CHARLES: Hello — who is this?
DIANA: It's Diana. Is that Snuggle-bum?
CHARLES: Snuggle bum? You've never called me that before ...
JAMES GILBEY: Yes it's me Squidgy?
CHARLES: Squidgy? What??! Er — I think we've got a crossed line.
SLOANE: Bloody cell phones. I'll call you back.
JAMES GILBEY: Okay Squidgy ...
CHARLES: She was talking to me! And who the bloody hell is that?
JAMES GILBEY: Hi — James Gilbey.
SLOANE: Hi James — I don't think we've met.
JAMES: You sound nice — do you fancy dinner some time?
SLOANE: Love to ... I know this lovely French place.
CHARLES: Do you two mind?
[cell phones explode]

DATE: 25 June + + + TIME: 11.24am
TARGET: THE BISHOP OF DURHAM + + + CALL FROM: GOD
DURHAM: Hello, Durham here, in a metaphysical sense.
GOD: It's Sunday morning. Why aren't you in Church?
DURHAM: Who is this?
GOD: It's God.
DURHAM: It can't be — you don't exist.
GOD: That's why I'm ringing. To prove that I do exist.
DURHAM: Not necessarily.
GOD: What do you mean?
DURHAM: You might be somebody pretending to be God.
GOD: I am God.
DURHAM: Prove it.
GOD: Umm...
DURHAM: Go on...
GOD: I've got a beard.
DURHAM: So's Rolf Harris. Doesn't make him a God.
GOD: Yes, but I'm omnipotent. I created the Heaven and Earth in six days, I can
send thunderbolts, make the sun-shine — all sorts of divine type things.
And ... um ... [THINKING] I've got a beard.
DURHAM: You said that one.
GOD: [RAISING VOICE] Look bollock-brain I'm God, alright!
DURHAM: Alright then — if you're God — as you say you are — how come there's so
much misery and suffering in the world? How come there's war and disease? How
come millions of innocent children are starving?
GOD: Um...
DURHAM: Well?
[LONG PAUSE]
GOD: Oh er — there's someone tapping on the telephone box.
I'd better go.
[CALL TERMINATED]

DATE: 24th June + + + TIME: 8.07pm
TARGET: FRANK BRUNO + + + CALL TO: HARRY CARPENTER
CARPENTER: Hello...
BRUNO: [FAINT VOICE] Hello, hello Harry?
CARPENTER: Frank, is that you?
BRUNO: [FAINT VOICE] Hello, I want to speak to Harry.
CARPENTER: Frank, it is Harry. [LOUDLY] You're holding the phone the wrong way
round.
BRUNO: I can't hear you.
CARPENTER: [LOUDLY] Turn the phone round Frank!
BRUNO: [FAINT VOICE] Harry, I can't hear you very well! I fink you've got the
phone the wrong way round again, Harry.
[CALL TERMINATED]

DATE: 24th June + + + TIME: All night
TARGET: GEOFFREY HOWE + + + [EXCERPT ONLY]
HOWE: ... and so that's why the standard railway gauge is 4 foot 8½ ins
and not Brunel's 7ft ¼in, which with its wider tracking meant
greater torque on inclines. Anyway thank you for listening
to me, its been really nice talking to you...
WOMAN: At the third stroke, it will be 12:01 precisely.
[CALL TERMINATED]

DATE: June 24th + + + TIME: 8.30pm
TARGET: BEN ELTON + + + CALL TO: STANDARD TANDOORI

WAITER: Hello Standard Tandoori — can I have your order please?
BEN ELTON: Hello I'd like to order an Indian meal please, not that I've got anything against Chinese food or indeed any other food from the Third World, and when I say Third World I am in no way implying that your society is in any way inferior to the West, the Indian sub-continent has a rich and varied culture which predates European so-called civilisation by hundreds of years, yes indeed...
WAITER: Could we just have your order please...
BEN ELTON: I would like a prawn korma please, not that I've got anything against prawns or any other crustaceans, they have every right to swim about and not be put in curries it just so happens that I prefer prawn kormas to chicken ones, no slight against chickens intended...
WAITER: Please — I have a lot of people waiting...
BEN ELTON: And I've just checked my fridge and there's nothing in it, yes absolutely nothing... [THREE HOUR ROUTINE, OMITTED HERE] So that's one prawn korma, a pilau rice, support the Tamils, you've been a puzzled Indian waiter, thank you goodnight!
[CALL TERMINATED]

DATE: June 25th + + + TIME: 5:17pm
TARGET: AGENT HARRIS + + +
CALL TO: SIR ROGER

HARRIS: Hello Boss — it's Harris here, the phone-tapper.
SIR ROGER: What do you want?
HARRIS: I'm worried about the PM. She doesn't seem to trust anyone.
SIR ROGER: What makes you say that?
HARRIS: I don't know — it's just a hunch. I think she may even be listening into _me_.
THATCHER: I am not.

DATE: 24th June + + + TIME: 11.27pm
TARGET: HER MAJESTY + + + CALL TO: PRINCE PHILIP

QUEEN: Hullo dear!
PHILIP: Who the bugger's that?
QUEEN: It's your wife, the Queen.
PHILIP: What do you want?
QUEEN: I'm just ringing to say it's your turn to turn the light out in the corridor.
PHILIP: Oh alright. Goodnight.
QUEEN: Goodnight. See you in the morning.
[CALL TERMINATED]

STARDATE: 71.4.76 + + + TIME: 6:20, WED NIGHTS
TARGET: MR SPOCK + + + CALL FROM: UNCONVINCING PLANET

SPOCK: Captain, we are picking up some interference.
KIRK: Explanation, Spock.
SPOCK: It would appear to be a primitive phone-tapping device employed by a being of lower intelligence.
KIRK: Establish visual contact with the leader.
UHURU: [GASPS] Captain! It's horrible.
SCOTT: Ah've seen some o' yon alien beasties in ma time, but never a muckle the like o' that!
KIRK: Hmmm... we'd better beam down. It could be dangerous. One of us may be reduced to a pile of rocksalt. I'll take Spock, McCoy and that bloke who's never appeared in the show before.
NEW BLOKE: So let's get this straight. The three main stars of the show are beaming down — plus me.
KIRK: Yes — any one of us could be zapped to a pile of steaming ash...
NEW BLOKE: Yeah — um actually my legs been playing up a bit — I'd rather stay behind if it's all the same to you.
[CALL TERMINATED NEW BLOKE CALLS AGENT]

DATE: June 24th + + + TIME: 11.47am
TARGET: J. R. HARTLEY + + + CALL TO: OLDE BOOKS

J. R. HARTLEY: Hello, have you got Fly Fishing by J. R. Hartley?
SHOPKEEPER: Oh not you again... Piss off you old goat.
[CALL TERMINATED]

DATE: June 24th + + + TIME: 12.55pm
TARGET: ROBERT MAXWELL + + + CALL TO: THE MANAGER, VERYBIG BANK PLC

MAXWELL: I want to extend my overdraft please...
MANAGER: You're not having another fifty pounds you miserable little student you...
MAXWELL: No you idiot it's me — Robert Maxwell and I want to borrow ten million zillion.
MANAGER: Oh sorry — certainly Mr Maxwell, would that be in addition to the thirteen quillion gillion fillion pounds you borrowed yesterday?
MAXWELL: Yes — I've already invested that in Icelandic Sun-Ray Lamps.
MANAGER: Oh good idea. Er — do you have any collateral for this new loan?
MAXWELL: A million shares in Just-made-it-up PLC which I've already bought with the profit I plan to make with Down-the-Plug-Hole Investments which I'm buying with this money you're going to lend me.
MANAGER: Oh er — that sounds fine then, we'll make it a round zillion.
MAXWELL: You're a wise man. I'll make you a suicidal bankrupt. Er — I mean a very rich man...
[CALL TERMINATED]

DATE: Nov. 5th + + + TIME: 5.34pm
TARGET: MANAGER, VERY BIG BANK PLC + + + CALL FROM: FRAUD SQUAD

FRAUD SQUAD: Hello it's the fraud squad here. Robert Maxwell has just topped himself by jumping off his yacht. You didn't lend him any money by any chance did you?
MANAGER: [SOUND OF GUNSHOT]
FRAUD SQUAD: Hello? Hello?
[CALL TERMINATED]

# SUNDAY SKIRT
## THE NEWSPAPER ADULTS READ

Europe's biggest office block found on wasteland

SEE PAGE 6

Sunday, June 35th     28p     THOUGHT: DUNNO

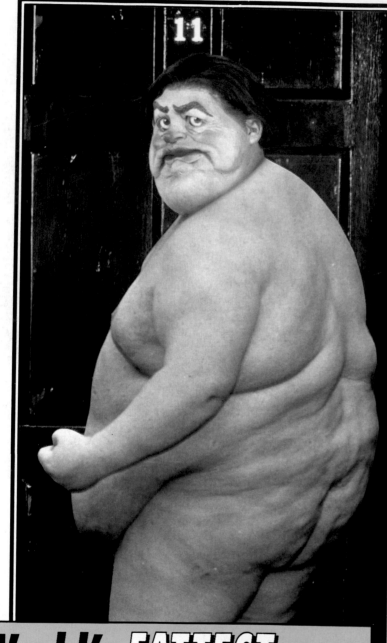

# GOVT TO TAX HEADS

● **A shock report sent to the Sunday Skirt reveals an incredible scheme to tax people for having... A HEAD!**

● The bizarre blue-print – known as the POLL TAX – means that a single mum will pay the same as the Duke of Westminster! But an expert CONFIRMED that the idea was genuine! "I am convinced it is the work of a madman," said Professor Bayliss

**FULL STORY INSIDE**

# World's FATTEST man to run economy!

See pages 8-14

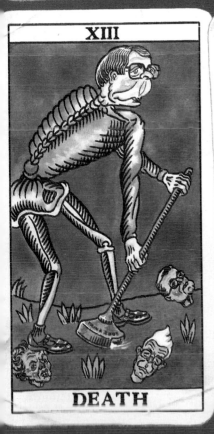

# The Last Cabinet Meeting

nd so it came to pass that when it was evening, they sat at table and broke bread, apart from John the Major, who shelled peas. And as they ate, a miracle was performed by Kenneth the Clerk, who turned twenty cans of lager into water. Well, eventually.

nd Margaret spake as they were eating, and said: "O Loyal and Trustworthy Friends!" And the others looketh a bit awkward, and did cough nervously. But Margaret did not see, and said: "Truly, I say to you that this very evening before the cock crows, one of you will betray me."

ne?" laugheth the others, and Douglas rose, saying: "Lo! Margaret! Your support is ver Margaret! For it is Written — on these ballot papers — that the time come for you to ascend and take your rightful place by the Lords." "Yea, b will return!" replied Margaret. "No y won't" chorused her old disciples. At which moment Margaret trotteth out

## GOSPEL ACCORDING TO S⁺ JOHN THE DULL

procession of Holy words. And she did take a bottle of wine and break it over Geoffrey's head saying "And this is your blood". Then she struck her forehead thrice upon Douglas's nose, saying: "And this is my body!"

And then came a great crowd of aides who laid hands on Margaret, and seized her. And Margaret said to the crowd: "Have you come out as against a robber?" And everyone thought about the Poll-tax, and said yes, they had. And Margaret screamed unto her disciples: "I cannot believe after twelve years you would forsake me and flee!" But none of them heard her, for they had all buggered off.

(cont'd from page 29) this illuminated sculpture was the most striking in the whole gallery. The bold statement of the simple word, 'Exit' placed so provocatively over the door, a twentieth century icon, a symbol proclaiming society's departure, a basic 'sine quo non' with an external illogicality denying yet inviting the observer's extended existence.

## A Nun writes

Being a nun, I find this portrait absolutely fascinating. But then a nun's life is rather dull, so I find most things "absolutely fascinating" – floorboards, bicycle spokes, El Dorado, etc.

Anyway, back to the painting. Perhaps we should know a little more about its background; it was painted by Leonardo Da Vinci; not the Leonardo Da Vinci of course, but his great great great great great great great grandson Leonardo Da Vinci the tenth Jr, who lives in Purley and prefers Speedway to painting but has to make a living.

The artist had just come out of his famous "blue" period, when he ran out of red and yellow paint but couldn't be arsed to go into town for some more, and was inspired to paint such a dramatic tableau by a call from Margaret Thatcher herself, who said: "I want a great religious painting about me, and I'll pay cash." Leonardo started work immediately, and didn't stop until it was finished almost forty minutes later.

The year was 1990 A.D., a year of enormous political turmoil, and the religious fervour of the era should not be played down. In those days Margaret Thatcher, the central figure in the painting, was genuinely believed to be a descendant of God, although only by herself, it must be said. So the betrayal is of enormous significance, and the artist has sought to bring out the intense emotions of his subjects by drawing their faces, something he usually can't be bothered to do. Even the numbers underneath have been completely covered over.

The artist himself always felt he'd left out the most important aspect of the work; his phone-number and availability, but you can find him in Yellow Pages under 'Pet Portraits'.

Dear Margaret,
As you can see, reaction to your resignation has
been the same the world over. I know you're not too
hot on speaking wop, so I've translated for you...

Your ever-loyal Press Officer

*Sir Brownose*

P.S. I'm pissing off to Scotland. John promised me
a nice fat retirement bonus in return for my help.

DIE WELT:
"Tragedy!"   ISSUE DATE: 29.11.90

# DIE ⊕ WELT

...IST OURS

# Kräppenfuhrerthätcherauson

Langenwordenkei... undvielenhyphenmussenhabenshortofbreathgegettenno-
...utneinlippensmackenkuhlgetastenthirstgequenchePepsi

ΕΘΝΟS:
"Come back
Maggie!"

# ΡΙΣΣ ΦΓΓ ΤΠΔΤCΠΞΡ

...φ ψου αρε τρψινγ το ωορκ ουτ
...ωηατ τηισ σαψσ, ψου μυστ βε
...αβσολουτλψ φυχκινγ μαδ. Ι
...ονλψ πυτ τηισ χοπψ ιν βεχαυσε
...τηοσε λαζψ βασταρδ ωριτερσ
...χουλδνΠτ βε βοτηερεδ το ωριτε
...ανψτηινγ φυννψ ορ οριγιναλ το
...φιλλ τηισ σπαχε. Ιφ ψου ηαωε

τρανσλατεδ τηισ φαρ ψουΠτ
οβωιουσλψ χραχκεδ μψ σιμπ...
χοδε, βυτ Ι βετ ψου χανΠτ ωο...
ουτ τηισ νεξτ βιτ. Σηε δεαδ ...
ψετι γονε α μιχκλε συχκλε ...
νιπρτ φδ νιππλε τιχκλερ.
τηατ σηουλδ κεεπ ψου βυσι...
π–θ/α+β²(πδxυ³)=π³–αν̅θ(λ̅...

LOS ARGENTINOS:
"Sadness as British P.M. resigns"
DATE: 29.11.90

# FJØRK ÖFF MÅGGIE!

"Well done Iron Lady, We'll miss you!"

SVENSKA DAGBLAT:

# NØTHING HÅPPENS IN STØCKHÖLM AGÄIN

Ole Ole

LE Monde :"Mitterand pays tribute to outstanding States woman"
DATE:

BEIJING ECHO :
"One day a wise woman governed a far-off
Land where the people
DATE:

(populace?) worshipped her, and anyway
she set off on a journey until she came
to a sort of crossroads...
meeting point, it doesn't
translate literally, but the
thing is, this woman stopped
and a monkey sprang out
of the bushes (temple?
pagoda?) no wait it wasn't
a monkey it was more the
sort of spirit of someone's
Ying and... look my
Cantonese is a bit rusty
but it certainly doesn't
say that an old cow
moved into No.10, shat on
the whole country and finally
got what she deserved."

# Le Mond

### Ze paper zat 'ates z'English. Pah!

## JEUDI 29 NOVEMBRE 1990

# Ferque oeuf merde-face

Sur le pont d'Avignon Monsieur Thibaut au bord de la
mere, Norway null points, voulez vous couchez avec moi? Les
Francais n'adore pas le Piat d'Or, pah pah pah! Camembert,
zut alors, Sacha Distelle. Papa? Nicole? Papa? Nicole? Papa?
Nicole? Papa Nicole PapaNicole Papanicolepapanicolepapan-
colepapanicole Shut up!!!

Les leadres des EC apres la resignation de la dragonne Anglais

¡El Gotcha!

Anos Madame Malvinas. Los Malvinas
belongas a Argentina y Malvinas. Los Malvinas
givos back Malvinas pl...
pleso pleso...

26

NGTCN POST

## Beavers put to the test

MINNESOTA, Tuesday – It was all go at
the Hooverdrome for the final quarterdown
of the semester as the Minnesota Beavers
took on the Denver Single-Cell Amoebas.
Hernandez switched the first play back on the
offense and sat down over the twenty two for
a triple linebacker with regular fries and anyway I'm busking it here – frankly I've never
understood it – but what happened is some
big gun an two yards and bumped into another guy and they both fell over. Then some
other guy threw it and they all ran after it and
the crowd seemed to go wild so I guess something must have happened but I couldn't
make head or tail of it. And then five minutes
later they did exactly the same thing only this
time it didn't count! Oh yeah, that reminds
me, they kept going into these weird huddles
and shouting out numbers and stuff and some
guy who must have been the coach kept
yelling into a microphone and let's be honest
it's a stupid game, if we hadn't invented it we
wouldn't have to pretend it's better than soc-
cer and I'm just looking forward to the World
Cup, I mean look at John Harkes, he's American and he scored for Sheffield Wednesday
in the final at Wembley...

## Pumpkin crop up

WISCONSIN, Monday – Farmers reported an increased yield of pumpkin in the Tup-
perware Basin area. "This is great news for
pumpkin-eaters" said delighted farmer
Hiram Seedbucket.

## English PM resigns

LONDON, Tuesday – London's Prime
Minister Margaret Th...
Re...

## WHAT CARAVAN

## ROAD TEST

# ALPINE 1500

When it comes to choosing a
caravan, there are many factors to
take into account: How powerful is
the car you own? How many
members of your family are you
likely to take with you? Will you be
touring at home or abroad? Do you
really want to spend a fortnight in a
godforsaken campsite next to
some bozos from Solihull who have
barbecues every night and sing Hi
Ho Silver Lining until three in the
morning, when you could be in a
nice comfortable hotel where the
nearest bath isn't a three mile walk
away and the water's actually hot
and they serve you a nice cooked
breakfast in the morning without
you having to get up at six and look
for a shop that sells milk on a
Sunday because the cartons you
left outside to cool in a bucket of
water have been eaten by a goat

"Sorry... cut this out by mistake, but at least
it doesn't slag you off like all the others... Oops."

The news of your resignation came as a great shock to me. It is with great sadness that I accept your resignation after so many years of devoted and loyal... Oh, let's cut the crap. When I planned it 6 months ago. Yippee! Good riddance you old bag, now gimme my bloody crown back.
— Geoffrey Howe

THATCHER ISN'T WORKING! GOD LUCK
NOT NOW SHE ISN'T! Charles + Maurice Saatchi
H.M. Queen

Well done Maggie! 1979–1990
That's 14 glorious years — no,
12, er... go some glorious years — 10,
13½
— '79 Kenneth Clarke

Great farewell party —
Margaret — sorry we didn't
invite you! Douglas Hurd

Nobody could
replace you
Margaret!
John Major

A nobody
did!
— Norman
Lamont

cheers Margaret
Just borrowed a bit
Card for a roach
— Ian Botham X.

There's no place in
Government for
power-crazed blods!
Michael
Heseltine

Best of luck
Princess Di.

who are we
suppose to pray
to now? George Carey
and your mates at the
church can pray-er!

**Graham's Vegetable Stall**

# 50p

← we all
→ had a
whip round
for you

GOODBYE, GOODBYE, GOODBYE,
FROM P.C. DIMBLEBY,
THE POLICEMAN WHO STOOD
ON YOUR DOORSTEP FOR
TEN YEARS AND NOT ONCE
DID YOU BRING ME A CUP
OF TEA, YOU TIGHT BASTARD...
"Steady Dim + Leb! Sargeant
Sorry Sir" P.C. DIMBLEBY.

THE WHOLE PARTY ARE MOTIVATED TO SEE YOU GO
SCRIBBLED THE BEST SELLING AUTHOR,
WAITING HIS BEST FICTION YET
— Jeffrey Archer

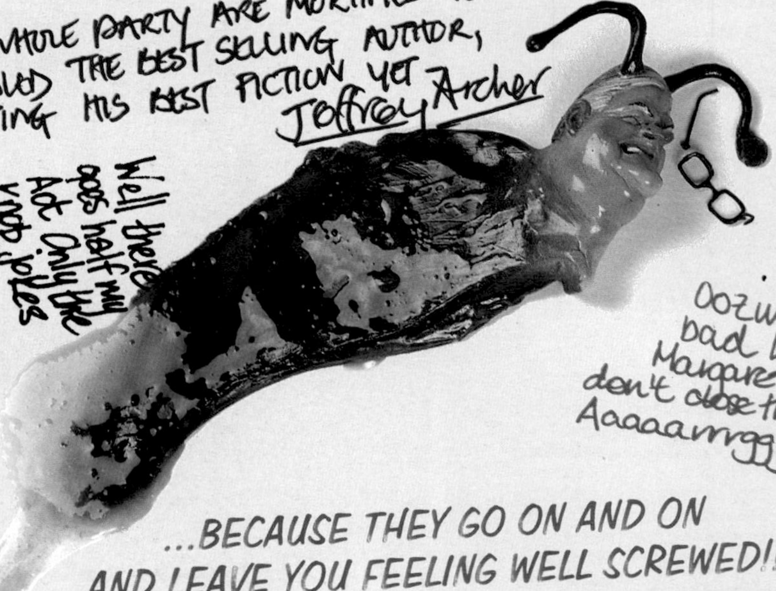

Well there
does half my
don't catch the card! No
Aaaaarrrgggghhh.

oozwugh.
bad luck
Margaret! No
don't close the car!
Aaaaarrrgggghhh.

...BECAUSE THEY GO ON AND ON AND ON
AND LEAVE YOU FEELING WELL SCREWED!!

Roses are red
Violets are blue
Black crow swoops,
putrifying badger,
Maggots in eye, kee-ow! kee-ow!
Dusk falls, vile earth rots.
— Ted Hughes, Poet Laureate.

BAD LUCK
MARGARET!
YOU WON'T
FIND ME BEING
DEPOSED BY
MY CHUMS!
YOURS
MIKAEL
GORBACHEV
I die.

Good ███, you ██████
█████████████████
█████████████ Peter Wright
███████████████ (spy catcher)
Can't think of
anything funny
to write —
Carla Lane

When I was asked to write
this message I was reminded of
my Sheffield boyhood and The
long cycle-ride to see Wednesday
versus United, clutching my purtin
butties as my grocer's bike rattled
over the cobble stones and er,
(cont. for twenty pages in
The Guardian.) Roy Hattersley

Can I interest you
in a Pension Scheme?
Robert Maxwell

I can't quite reach the table — Colin Moynihan

Best
Wish
Maggie
Brian
Clow

# Johnny 'Peacrusher' Major

## THE ULTIMATE ACCOUNTANT

NUMERO TEN-O

my world-champion successor – <u>NOT</u> !

## Fact File

Johnny 'Peacrusher' Major strikes fear and terror into the heart of anyone who sees him coming towards them at a cocktail party. His sworn enemy is John 'Sensible' Smith, although he won his current title by beating the ultimate WINDBAG.

**Age:** Middle    **Colour:** Grey

**Eyes:** Four    **Statistics:** Loves them

**Background:** Grew up wrestling with bought ledger accounts in the swamps of Orpington

**Known for:** Dithering

**Favourite quote:** "Er – can I get back to you on that?"

**Top wrestling trick:** Frequently leaves his opponents unconscious with his trademark move of 'talking to them'

**Titles held:** 'Accountancy Made Easy', 'The AA Book of Moss', 'The Art of 'Creo-soteing'

WEENY WILLY CONFEDERATION

WWC

## ROOM ON MY OWN

# MARGARET THATCHER

Since retiring suddenly as Prime Minister of Britain in November 1990, Margaret Thatcher has divided her time between her home in the centre of London, and upstairs in her home in the centre of London. "It's very convenient living here" she says, "as most of my friends live nearby in the radiator".

The first thing she did when she arrived was rip out the fireplaces, knock through several party walls and pull the floorboards up. The existing tenants called the police from the bathroom, where they had locked themselves in.

Margaret's favourite room is the front room, which she uses as lounge, office, bedroom, and sometimes toilet. She refused to let go of a few things from Downing Street, like the front door frame.

One of the most striking features of the room is the fascinating collection of empty whisky bottles. They are all the same brand and are displayed in a casual, almost chaotic way around the floor and shelves of the room. One of the more exotic *objets d'art* is a traditional Haitian figurine which looks remarkably like John Major, and also serves as a pin cushion.

For the net curtains she's chosen a dusty-grey tone, a common theme in the room. There is also a love of plants here. Fascinating species of funghi of all colours are lovingly grown on specially left saucepans of old baked beans.

The unusual scent of the room is from a homemade *pot pourri* of Felix cat-litter, damp towels, and a piece of old rock salmon arranged in a newspaper. One of her hobbies is obviously making cheese and yoghurt on the stairs. "Yes I must wash those milk bottles out" she muses. A frequent feature of the room is a roaring fire; usually caused by Margaret drying her vests over the paraffin heater.

She is keen to remind me of her former achievements. "I used to be Prime Minister, you know", she comments, repeating the statement for good measure. I asked her about her busy schedule: "Well it starts at about eight am with breakfast TV - then at ten it's Kilroy followed by Rainbow and Home and Away. I usually fall asleep during Open University".

She also has to read the never-ending stream of correspondence that comes through her letterbox, and knows everything about pizza deliveries, mini-cab numbers and special offers on carpet cleaning. But what does she like to do with her spare time? Several hours later I tap her gently on the shoulder. "Oh, hello - do come in".

Where does she see herself going next? "To the bathroom. You couldn't help me up could you? I get so giddy" she quips.

## INTERVIEW BY NORMELLA FOWLER

# ...MY QUOTES ARE OFTEN TAKEN OUT OF CONTEXT...

## CHESS

### Horace Acne

This intriguing game was recently played out between the Ukranian Grandmaster **M Dozedoffavich** and **I Sleep**, British Grandmaster of the Grand Lodge of East Grinstead...

**1 c4 c62 e4 e5 3 Nf3 Qa5**
White is now in a good position to adjust his glasses.

**4 Be2 f5 5 exf5 e4 6 Ng5 Qxf5!**
High drama as Black responds by chewing one of the little toggles on his anorak.

**7 Qe2 ub40 8 r2d2 c3po 9 e246 e321 (antioxidant) 10 bbc2 m25**
White forgets whose move it is.

**11 Zzzzzzzzzzzz**
Black falls asleep.

**12 ....Ahem!**
White flicks bogey at Black's Queen. Black wakes up.

**13 F\*@#'&@ @#©!**
Black accuses White of cheating.

**14 fU2!!**
White counters the accusation and goes on the attack

**15 fist x jaw 16 boot x bollocks!**
White presses home the advantage.

**17 Chess set x floor**
Black goes home and refuses to be White's friend any more

**Final position:**

**This week's puzzle:** Why do people play chess?

---

Whi... ...g wrong with the top track for working horses? (7)
**21** Call to grab pole and tie up (4)
**22** At ood a uniform covers nothing (6)
**23** Leather around tips of ladies footwear (4)
**24** Tranquilliser for Sailor Bill in grip of a convulsion (9)
**27** Glaciation stage starts to retreat in sunny spells (4)
...all for highland cow test when tail drops off (4)

## BRIDGE

### Marjorie Doyley

This intriguing hand was recently played out at the Blyth Hamiltons' regular Tuesday night bridge party...

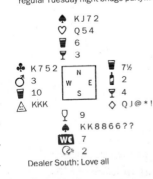

♠ K J 7 2
♡ Q 5 4
♧ 6
♢ 3

♣ K 7 5 2    ♠ 7½
♂ 3    ♡ 2
♧ 10    ♧ 4
△ KKK    ♢ Q J @ \* !

♧ 9
♡ KK 8 8 6 6 ??
**WC** 7
♧ 2

Dealer South; Love all

|West|North|East|South|
|---|---|---|---|
|1 ◇|pass|1 ♡|Whose bid is it? Oh – pass.|
|1 ♠|pass|3 ◇|Are aces high or low?|
|pass| |pass?!!!| |

Don't start   Oh, for crying
George   out loud!
**North:** Let's get on with the game shall we?
**East:** You keep out of this.
**South:** Twenty one! Blackjack
**North:** You're making a bloody fool of yourself dear.
**South:** Um... More prawn Vol-au-vents anyone?
**West:** Yes please Emma.
**East:** Oh yes, wouldn't do to 'pass' on the food, would it darling?
**North:** Look, this is silly
**West:** I think Roger's got a point darling.
**East:** Oh that's right, take Roger's side.
**West:** You're a fine one to talk. Don't think I haven't noticed the way you've been gawping at Emma's tits all night.
**South:** Marjorie!
**West:** Well it's true
**East:** Downs remainder of whisky.
**North:** Look, I think we've all had a bit too much to drink. Why don't we
**South, West & East:** Shut up!
**North** goes through to the kitchen.
**East:** Perhaps it would be better if we left.
**South** kicks **East's** leg under the table.
**East:** Actually, Emma and I have an announcement to make.
**South:** Yes, we've decided to run off with each other.
**West** cries, screams, swears and ends up in bed with **North**

## COURTHOUSE COMPREHENSIVE SCHOOL
### Saterday 15th July 2pm

...o you have any unwanted
...oks, chairs, desks, science
...s, roofs, teachers? Pleas...
...thing, we're desperate
...20p would be a star...

Recycled paper. Same every week.

# HE LOCAL
# advertiser
## INCORPORATING CAT-LITTER LINING

# ...e Council are
# ...ry good

By our head - well alright, only - reporter, **WANDA BETTERJOB**

The Council are very good – that's the message from a new report by the local council, sent exclusively to the Local Advertiser.

**THE REPORT** goes on to say "Paste this straight into your two-bit rag you sad excuse for a journalist." Council leaders are pleased that this latest report vindicates them after the opposition report we published last week under the headline "The Council are very bad..."

It was sunny this week so ...ere's a gratuitous picture of a pretty girl in a T-shirt

## VICIOUS ATTACK ON PENSIONER

A VICIOUS attack on a pensioner was probably carried out somewhere in the borough this week, writes a lazy journalist. The attacker was probably wearing a bomber jacket, jeans and trainers and would no doubt have got away with less than ten pounds in cash, or thereabouts. Anyway, that's enough hard news, now for thirty pages of uninteresting adverts ... carpets, clutche... shelving...

*...my correspondence now.
...the post-bag of a VERY
IMPORTANT lady*

# MARKUPP & LYER
## ESTATE AGENTS AND VALUERS

**22, BOARD UP ROAD, LONDON SW4**

## 10, POSH MEWS, DULWICH SE64

This completely detached family residence is situated in the increasingly popular, just-been-thought-up-by-the-estate-agents North Dulwich Triangle. There are several excellent local schools, at least one of which remains open. Transport facilities are excellent, with very few buses to annoy the chauffeur.

The property has a new roof and the walls have recently been plastered, as have the present occupiers. There is a large garden with a two hundred mile exclusion zone. The property would benifit from some re-decoration, and an exorcism.

* FIVE BEDROOMS    * BATHROOM

* LIVING ROOM    * TOILET

* KITCHEN    * NO CHAIN

## THE ACCOMMODATION COMPRISES:

**EXTERIOR** Imposing driveway with large neon sign: "This way Mark"

**ENTRANCE HALL** Leading to stairs, leading to... well upstairs obviously, but anyway let's do this bit first...

**LIVING ROOM** 28' x 20', Original Victorian fireplace with own chimney-sweep.

**DINING ROOM** 20' x 18', With walk-in drinks cabinet.

**LIBRARY** 17'8 x 14', Never been used.

**UTILITIES ROOM** Sold off.

**KITCHEN** Fully fitted, with film crew and Lloyd Grossman saying "I wondurr who-wuh li-urves hee-urr?"

**MASTER BEDROOM** 24' x 17'6, Padded; bed and manacles to remain.

**BEDROOM 2** 8" x 3½", Single; Dennis to remain.

**BEDROOM 3/4** Fitted wardrobe, pulls down to become broken wardrobe.

**BATHROOM** 5000 volt bath; 'His' and 'Hers' razor points.

**TOILET** With mirror (in handy tear-off sheets).

**GARDEN** Delightful portcullis, leading to moat, well-stocked with hammerhead sharks. Ornamental pond with ducking stool. Lovely lawn with one or two freshly dug bits and some sort of bonfire with charred bones, it was probably just a barbeque.

~~£240,000~~ £2.23p
~~£600,000~~
**PRICE ~~£700,000~~* - NO OFFERS**
**************************

*Anyone Interested*

* Price includes carpets (slight teeth marks). Lightbulbs negotiable, say 20p each. Must be seen - or the boys from 'C' Division will come round and beat you to a messy pulp.

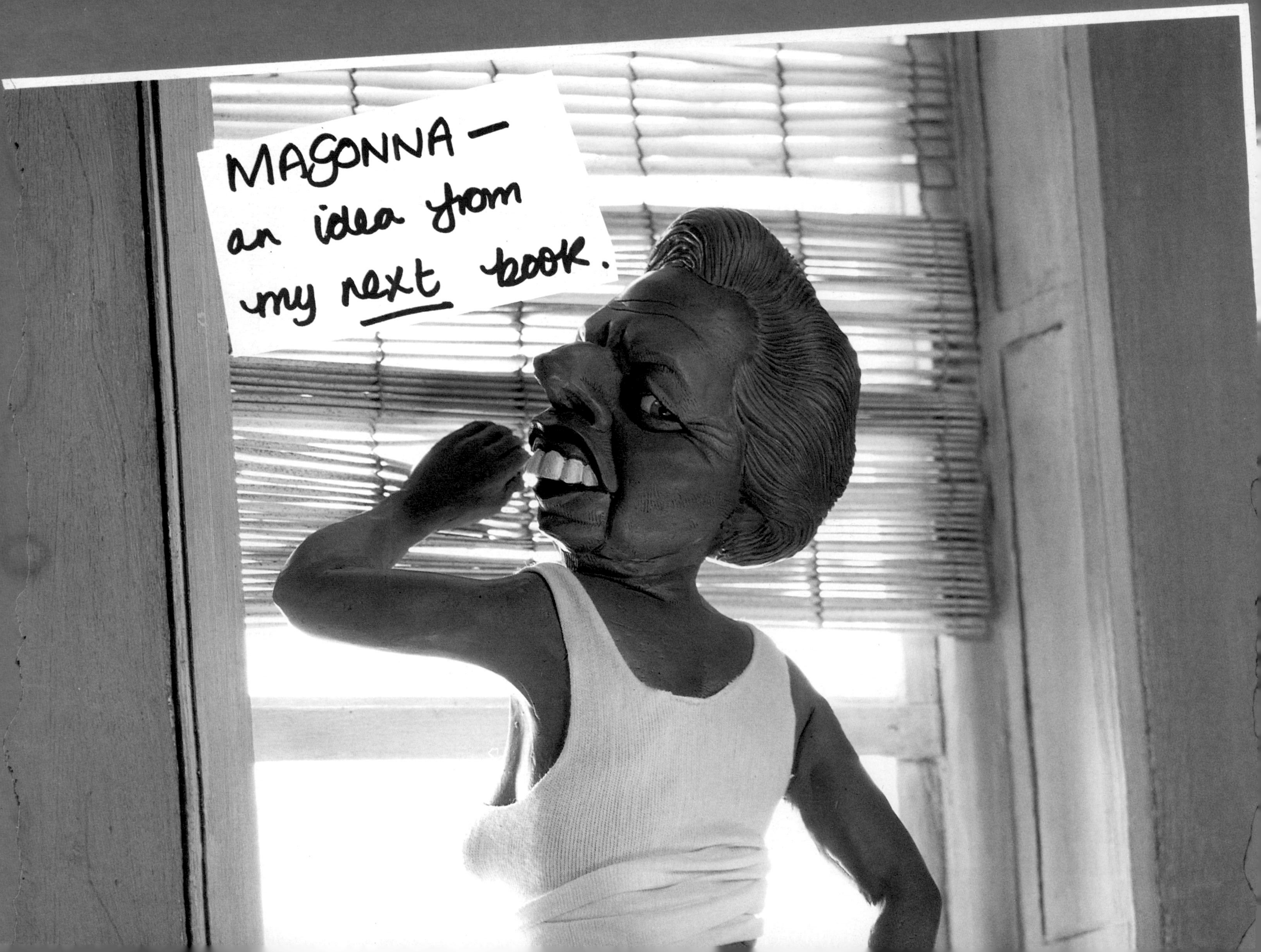
MAGONNA –
an idea from
my next book.

## End-of-the-Showcall
Directory of very available piss-artistes

### Unique international act
She's outrageous, she's outspoken, she's stark raving bonkers

# MARGARET THATCHER
Catchphrase: "Rejoice, rejoice"

### Many talents...
- Own original madcap material
- Unique silly walk
- Funny patter including brand new hilarious 'Maastricht' routine
- Once had own show on TV (The Conservative Party Political Broadcast)
- Has released novelty single 'The Gettysburg Address' (Most copies still available)

### Ideal for...
- Party Conferences ● American lecture tours
- Stag nights ● Kiddies parties ● Pantos
- Cruises ● Prime Minister, if asked

Now booking! Some dates still available

### SOLE REPRESENTATION: THATCHER FOUNDATION

**Can appear with handbag..**

**...or without handbag!**

THE PROPHESIES OF NOSTRADAMUS

235

From the land of the vikings
shall come four minstrels,
Whose trousers shall
o'erspill their shoes,
And they shall sing of Fernando
and the Dancing Queen.

236

And a fierce warrior known as
Thatchler shall lead Angle-land,
And the Franks and Huns shall be
smitten by her handbag,
With fire and combustion, the Island
of the sheep shall be reconquered.
And the Welsh Man of Wind shall
be thrice defeated,
And after her voluntary retirement
she shall be asked back to be
Prime Minister again 'cos that divvy
John Major is such a wet blanket
and nowhere near as good as her.

237 It is Written!
I'll be back!

Printed by M. Thatcher, 1993